The Life and Times of the Cricket Bat Willow

Limited edition
No. 106

ANGLIAN WILLOW SERVICE

4 GENERATIONS OF EXPERTISE

VAT REG. No. 247 1471 64

Consultant Specialists: D. A. WATLING
G. S. WATLING

19th October, 1998.

J. Ferris, Esq.,
10 Field Close,
West Haddon,
Northants,
NN6 7AB

Dear Mr. Ferris,

I am sorry it was necessary for you to return your copy of "The Lifc and Times of the Cricket Bat Willow" which seems to have sustained damage somewhere along the production line.

Mr. Watling has signed a replacement copy for you with the wish that you enjoy reading it. He also relished your remarks on bat sizing - 'more power to your elbow' springs to mind.

Kind regards.

Yours sincerely,

V. Watling (Mrs)
Watling Enterprises.

Enc:

Registered Office:
4 CHEVERS HALL COTTAGE CHELMSFORD ROAD HIGH ONGAR ESSEX CM5 9NX
Tel/Fax: (01277) 363950

The Life and Times of the Cricket Bat Willow

By Douglas A. Watling

ISBN 0 9534041 0 2

Written in collaboration with and published by
Hassan Mughal,
1 Norfolk Chase,
Warfield, Berkshire, RG42 3XN
Tel/Fax: 01344 426509
E-mail: imperial@lineone.net

Printed by BAS Printers Limited,
Over Wallop, Hampshire

CONTENTS

This book is dedicated to three special people without whom we would never have made it . . .

My lovely wife Val who nearly drove me mad with the incessant chatter of her typewriter as she strove to keep up with my writing and for putting up with my impatience.

My ghost writer and friend, Hassan Mughal, who chivvied me unmercifully until I agreed to write the book, who has supported my decisions, and who has worked so hard to produce the book.

My Dad who taught me all I know.

ACKNOWLEDGEMENTS

The author acknowledges with gratitude the very generous help he has received with certain photographic plates.

Dr. John Gibbs of the Research Department of the Forestry Authority

Dr. John Turner of the School of Biological Sciences of the University of East Anglia, Norwich, Norfolk

Mr. Michael Wortley of the Estates Department, Essex County Council, Chelmsford

Mr. Ned Tabor of Fennes Estate, Bocking, Essex

Mrs. Margaret Tabor of Bovingdon Hall Estate, Bocking, Essex

Dillon Bryden, Freelance International Photographer, London (0802-367373)

Messrs. Warsop-Stebbing of Danbury, Essex

Imperial Bats of Warfield, Berkshire (Hassan Mughal)

and

Mr. Neil Gray of Messrs. Gray-Nicolls, Robertsbridge, East Sussex, for the loan of cricket bats.

Introduction

The beautiful game of Cricket is blessed with many heroes, most of them visible, such as exciting batsmen, bowlers of alarming pace or mesmerising merchants of googly and wrist spin. Yet in the annals of the game there are some who are equally important but visible only to a few. One such legend is Douglas Arthur Watling.

Doug, as he is affectionately known, gives the reader a unique insight into the complex science of growing *Salix Alba Caerulea*, the highly vaunted **CRICKET BAT WILLOW**. This science has become Doug's lifelong work. He is today widely acknowledged by all concerned in the world of cricket and cricket bat making as the foremost authority on Cricket Bat Willow in the world.

Doug's willow has been used by icons of cricket for many decades, and this book is the culmination of knowledge passed down through four generations of willow growers in the Watling family. It is a definitive authority on the science of Cricket Bat Willow, a work of unparalleled insight, glimpsing at times into the romance of cricket and the cricket bat. It is a worthy testament to the man who, from his hundred-year-old home near Ongar, Essex, has decided to tell the reader about this fascinating species of wood, which has provided adulation for cricket fans of all ages.

Foreword

THE AUTHOR

Four Generations of *Salix Alba Caerulea* **Expertise**

Douglas Arthur Watling – Born 9th January 1922

Son of Douglas Charles Watling (1899–1971)

Son of Thomas Watling (1847–1902)

Son of Ishmael Watling (1813–1884)

Son of Robert Watling (1790–1834)

I was born in Woodbridge in the East Anglian County of Suffolk on 9th January 1922. At that time my Father, Douglas Charles, was involved with Wisdens, the sports manufacturers of London and Penshurst, Kent, in the capacity of Willow Buyer. This was a fact of particular significance, as my grandfather, Thomas, ran a business as a general timber merchant with premises located on the Quay at Woodbridge, plying his trade along the East Coast by barge.

His involvement with willow was of even greater significance, as he was witness to the inception of trade in the first cricket bat willows, including probably witnessing the largest ever cricket bat willow tree to be felled at Lavenham in Suffolk.

I also recall my Father speaking of a giant willow tree felled at Boreham in Essex in the late 1800's, which made in excess of a thousand bats and measured about a hundred feet in length. This was originally planted, I believe, in the early 1800's. Naturally, we do not see many trees like that nowadays, but I myself felled a tree with 600 bats in the West Bergholt area of Essex. The dearth of such trees can be attributed to the fact that there is a very high demand for Cricket Bat Willow, and frankly, we cannot afford to leave them to reach that sort of age. Today's trees are usually felled at about 16 years of age, producing some 40 to 50 bats. Yes, we do get the odd exception, but very few and far between.

It is interesting to marvel at the super efficiency of modern day transportation of all manner of items, whatever they may be. There was no such transportation available in those hard, austere times. The chief mode of transportation used for moving willows was the primitive, but effective, timber wagon. The mainstay of cargo transport relied not on engine power, but the raw power of four to six horses. Initially timber was hauled direct to Woodbridge by these wagons and later by rail or barge.

Willow timber would be carried in the form of a 'round' or a 'roll' measuring 30 inches in length, and of varying diameters ranging from 18 inches to 3 or 4 feet, dependent upon the years of growth of any particular tree.

The town of Woodbridge, whilst being my birthplace also nearly saw my demise. One Sunday afternoon, I was walking along the Quay with my sister and younger brother. We sometimes walked quite close to the edge. On this occasion I toppled off the Quay into about 12 feet of water and was about go down for the last time, when a passer-by dressed in sartorial Sunday elegance, plunged in and pulled me, a very frightened and bedraggled 9-year-old into the relative safety of a nearby barge.

At the tender age of 14, I joined my Father at a time when travel was restricted to horse and cart, bicycle (axes and crosscut saws tied to the crossbar) and a very early Hillman Coventry with a bullnose similar to the later Morris. Other tools of the trade were Ash wedges and a lot of sheer 'guts'!

Axes and saws were razor sharp so you can imagine the hazards involved in not only using them, but carrying them on the bicycle. I still bear the scars of early attempts of the process known as 'chopping out', about which, more later.

Those early times were indeed tough, because you were required to exert a great deal of physical effort simply getting to work, dependent on the weather. Indeed, I

Fig. 1 Doug Watling and bicycle complete with axes, crosscut saw and wedges

remember cycling from Colchester to Harwich, a distance of some 19 miles, with all the necessary 'paraphernalia' of work attached to both me and machine, working 'till dark, then repeating the journey homewards. It took single-mindedness and a lot of guts.

Willow trees which could be considered suitable for making good cricket bats, were relatively scarce in those days. There did not exist an 'industry' as we know it today. The average price we paid for a tree was £5 or even less. Those were dark days, hard days, tough days. We learnt by our mistakes – we had to – there were no experts then, no such thing as authority or precedent in the field of cricket bat willow expertise. We literally had nothing to go on; no one had previously trod the ground that we were about to embark upon. This lack of expertise gave me the opportunity to harness each experience and add to a slow and laborious learning curve.

Even as late as 1946, I remember meeting with senior members of the Forestry Commission who readily admitted that they knew very little about the Cricket Bat Willow trade.

In those early days, much was unknown about what was dubbed in local Suffolk parlance as the "Willer Business". They called my Father the "WILLER KING" as a result of his involvement in the trade. On many occasions, the felling of willow trees would attract large crowds, who became fascinated with what was becoming regular event. They watched the timber being split into 'cake like' sections, which were then chopped into rough shapes and further refined by using a traditional drawknife, the whole process being called 'chopping and drawing', about which, more later.

With this sketchy, but brief insight into the early beginnings of my involvement in the willow trade, as well as my family genealogy, I believe the pattern for my later years was moulded.

My father died in 1971. He was not a wealthy man in financial terms, but what he did leave me was an unparalleled wealth of knowledge, a practical grounding and an intimate knowledge of ***SALIX ALBA CAERULEA*** – the authentic Cricket Bat Willow. I took over the reins of the business and renamed it ***ANGLIAN WILLOW SERVICE*** – a name which remains to this day. I write and travel, conducting lectures and shows throughout the cricket playing countries of the world on this business that has become my life's work. I am recognised world wide as the leading authority on the subject of cricket bat willow. Today the business supplies cricket willow to all parts of the world, including Australia for the manufacture and making of cricket bats. I consider it my good fortune to be able to pass this vast array of knowledge harnessed and harboured from all those decades to my son Geoffrey, who joined the firm in 1992 as a partner. He is fully involved in all aspects of the business, and will assume the reins upon my retirement, which date will be established later.

Fig. 2 Douglas A. Watling

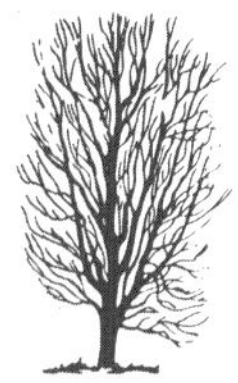

CHAPTER ONE

In the Beginning – Propagation of Cricket Bat Willow Via Sett Beds

The entire process by which a cricket bat eventually becomes an entity from the *Caerulea* species has been tackled previously, but in the main by arboriculturists. The subject has not been addressed with any modicum of expertise, partly due to the fact that there has not been available the specialist level on this matter. I hope to give both a general and specific treatment to *Caerulea* from the standpoint of expertise that I have gained through the years of experience touched upon in the previous section.

This book will, therefore, appeal more generally to those of the farming fraternity, upon whose land the majority of Cricket Bat Willow is grown. Nevertheless, it will also be of value to those who play the game and are students and viewers of batsmanship, because so many myths shroud the Cricket Bat Willow. Why does this bat drive better than another? Does colouring have anything to do with it? There are so many tales, stories and the so called 'sages' on the properties of the Cricket Bat Willow, that it is indeed somewhat of a minefield. I will explain in some detail, the consequences of growing and nurturing this species, which do in fact have a bearing on the manner in which the final product is fashioned.

To understand *Salix Alba Caerulea* we need to establish its position in the hierarchy of the 90 or so species of willow that frequent the countryside of the United Kingdom. Some are propagated, whilst others thrive as uncontrolled "weeds" adding to the general vegetation of the landscape.

There are two particular species of willow that we ought to identify first, because they grow sufficiently well and follow the general pattern closely enough, to be associated with 'cricket bat making', because they have actually been the subject of experimentation and although they have been found wanting in acceptable circles, they are still used by third world countries in the making of cheap cricket bats. Some of the reasons for using these two species are, as I will discuss later, predominantly economic ones.

The first of these species, which results in poor cricket bats, is the *Salix Fragilis*. In our circles we refer to it as the "curly bark". This is so because the outer bark takes on a "curly" look, somewhat unsymmetrical and irregular. This is opposite to our principle subject, the *Caerulea*, which has a regular and symmetrical or "close bark".

The second of these species is the *Salix Viridis* (Fig. 4). This is commonly referred to in the trade as the "open bark". The outer bark is coarse, open in formation and gives rise to a strong green serrated leaf. This is a larger leaf than both the *Fragilis* (Fig. 3) and *Caerulea* (Fig. 5), who both by contrast, have a more delicate, somewhat smaller leaf with a silver green surface.

Fig. 3 Salix Fragilis *or Curly Bark*

Fig. 4 Salix Viridis *or Open Bark*

Fig. 5 Silver green leafage of Salix Alba Caerulea

What then makes these two species unsuitable for cricket bat making? Why are they not used by modern bat makers in the process which produces standard size cricket bats? The simple and short answer is that **they are too heavy**. This is due to the basic high density of wood that these species pack as opposed to the much lighter density of wood in the *Caerulea*.

Let us examine the argument in some detail. If a bat maker takes an identical mass of *Salix Fragilis*, *Salix Viridis* and *Caerulea*, he would discover that in spite of this, there would be a significant difference in the individual weights of the specimens in question. It is possible, in approximate ratios, that all three pieces of wood, all at the same stage of drying (bearing similar levels of moisture content), would weigh probably as follows: The two former species might typically show a weight in excess of 3 lbs. The latter, *Caerulea*, would almost certainly culminate in a cricket bat ranging between 2 lbs 6 ozs to 2 lb 10 ozs in weight.

This scenario can be equated to the real life 'on the field' predicament constantly brought into sharp focus by a typical batsman about to contemplate facing a delivery from a Test Class fast bowler. In many cases, the hostile fast bowling tactics of modern bowling armouries necessitate targeting the body of the batsman, as well as his wicket. This controversial issue has been the subject of fierce debate over decades, and yet is specifically relevant to our argument. Let us assume the batsman is at the crease ready to face a fast bowler hurling a red leather missile at his wicket (or him!) at something approaching 100 mph. How will he react? Indeed, more to the point, which of the three bats will be an effective defence? The answer is an elementary one and does not require great thought to work out that if he is using a lighter cricket bat he can get bat to ball very much quicker and save both his wicket and his legs. In fact the debate regarding the weight of a cricket bat is a wide ranging and far reaching one.

Indeed we can quote a very famous West Indian batsman who used to use a Gray-Nicolls Dynadrive (Fig. 7), a bat which has an optimum playing weight of some 2 lbs 10 ozs (considered by Test batsmen to be on the heavy side) and with which he had only a moderate performance at the wicket. He was persuaded to change to a Gray-Nicolls Scoop 2000 (Fig. 8), a lighter bat altogether weighing approximately 2 lbs 6 ozs to 2 lbs 7 ozs, with spectacular results at the wicket. The statistics reveal an astonishing tale. World Records were shattered in 1994, when he smashed his way to a new Highest Test Score of 375 at St. John's, Antigua. Just a few weeks later, he stormed into the record books again by hitting a massive 501 not out – an all time World Record in First Class cricket (Figs. 6 & 9). That's right – it was the great Brian Lara, considered by some to be **the** greatest batsman of all time. Those who have seen Lara in action enthuse about the range and multitude of shots that he plays. Some of those shots would never even be contemplated using a heavier bat, let alone executed in the style he plays them. There are many other examples, but as I have said before, the debate is endless.

Fig. 6 Brian Lara celebrating at Edgbaston

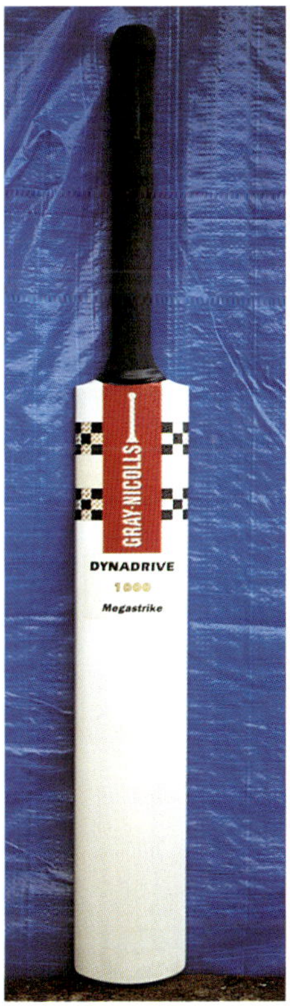

Fig. 7 Gray-Nicolls Dynadrive

Fig. 8 Gray-Nicolls Scoop 2000

Fig. 9 Signed commemorative bat

Fig. 10 Prime example of Salix Alba Caerulea

Thus, for the moment ends our incursion on the issue of the *Fragilis* and the *Viridis*. We must now turn our attention to the real matter in hand, the propagation of *Salix Alba Caerulea*, the definitive Cricket Bat Willow. The process is the same for all three species quoted.

Imagine, if you will, a superb example of *Caerulea* (Fig. 10) approximately 15 years old, straight boled for 10 feet without blemish, having a good symmetrical head, parading a full and healthy set of leaves all resulting from a vibrant unencumbered growth.

Three minutes, with a modern chain saw, would see this prime "ripe" specimen on the ground ready (Fig. 11), firstly, for cutting into 28 inch lengths (usually four, although sometimes three lengths dependent on the length of the initial Sett when planted) (Fig. 12) and, secondly, clearing the top and burning the brushwood. In normal circumstances, this would lead us on to other processes of cutting and preparing the willow, but since we are endeavouring to demonstrate the principle of propagation, we must needs examine the matter further.

Fig. 11 "Ripe" specimen on ground

Fig. 12 Cutting into 28 inch lengths

The top branches are naturally of varying sizes from quite large to small (say 3 to 4 inches in diameter) and it is from these smaller branches our "step one" commences.

Fig. 13 Branch used for Sett Stake

Fig. 14 Chopped and prepared Sett Stakes

Taking one of these branches then cut a 3 feet length of 3 inch to 4 inch diameter. Chop or saw a point on the end nearest the point of original attachment to the tree, thus . . . (Fig. 13).

The illustration *left* shows what now becomes a "Sett Stake" and is the first stage of establishing a Sett Bed (Fig. 14).

A few pointers here to keep you on the right lines and enable you to get a successful start:

1) Prepare your area first by thoroughly tilling and scarifying to obtain a fine tilth and to free it of any unwanted weeds. Yes, we do know they'll rear their ugly heads again, but that is one of

the reasons we plant 4 feet apart. This gives the "stake" room to grow and also allows easy access for rotavating in season to keep the weeds down and away from the young, sprouting Setts that will very soon appear as the "stake" commences to grow. We have now established our Sett Bed and providing the "stakes" have been properly planted (i.e. deep enough), in nice straight rows, in well prepared "clean" ground, we can look forward to a prolific crop of "Setts" over a period of 3 to 4 years.

There are, however, the following provisos to be put into effect.

2) The whole "Bed" must be guarded against rabbits by erecting wire netting, taking care not to leave any gaps or holes, with particular attention to the gate area. Rabbits allowed to wander unchecked amongst such choice "sett stakes" can strip the equivalent of an acre within the space of a mere two weeks. A further deterrent is the spiral guard, since these "stakes" are also regarded as lovely chewing posts for rabbits and their big brothers, the hares! They are also very fond of the fresh new shoots on the "stake" tops (Fig. 15).

Fig. 15 Younger Sett Bed

Assuming you propose to plant such an area, commence to plant these "stakes" at intervals of 4 feet in a symmetrical row or rows. As I mentioned before, the length of a Sett Stake is 3 feet and they must be planted ensuring that about half of its length is inserted below ground level. Further care must be taken in "firming" the soil back around the stake so that it is stable.

Moving on some 3 to 4 years, our Sett Bed should now be a mass of long, straight, slender pole-like growths (Fig. 16).

Fig. 16 3–4-year-old Sett Bed with a mass of pole like growth

These should be about 10 to 12 feet long with smaller shoots growing along its entire length with a healthy head of leaves shaping the top into a mini tree head.

A "stake" may produce anything up to five or seven of these "Setts", for that is what they are (Fig. 17).

Fig. 17 Stake with 5–6 growing Setts

We now come to the point of harvesting our crop, and there are two ways to do this:

1) By individual selection, that is picking only the best, the straightest and cleanest, or
2) By completely heading the stake, or in other words cutting all the growth at the top of the stake. THE STAKE ITSELF MUST NOT BE CUT. This stake will grow on again and produce three crops over a period of 10 years, after which it will need replacing with a new "stake", and the entire process begins again (Fig. 18).

Fig. 18 Established Sett Bed recently cropped

Fig. 19 Selecting of individual Sett from Sett Bed

It is my personal preference to completely head the stake, for the following reasons:

A) The system of picking out just the best setts leaves the stake littered with a head of secondary growth which certainly keeps the stake busy, but will never produce much more than what we call "pins" or small setts, plus unproductive secondary growth. This method simply holds up the propagationary system unnecessarily (Fig. 19).

B) Complete heading clears the stake for the process of reproduction over the next 3 to 4 years to the next cropping (Fig. 20).

Using this second process of cutting all the growth from the growing stake, you will find you have a miscellany of straight setts, crooked growths and small brushwood. By selecting out all the setts and burning the brushwood as a matter of policy, we are now left free to concentrate on the crop itself.

Fig. 20 Complete heading of Sett Stakes

Using an ultra sharp axe, or billhook, trim all or any secondary growth from the stem of the sett. Always trimming upwards (never downwards) with clean strokes, continue until leaving eventually a full head of growth on the top of the sett (Fig. 21).

Finally, to allow for ease of transporting and handling, setts are tied at each end in bundles of 10, thus enabling us to speed to our planting site (Fig. 23).

Fig. 21 Trimming up Sett

Fig. 22 Completed Sett ready for planting

Fig. 23 Bundled Setts

CHAPTER TWO

Planting, Guarding, Care and Attention of Setts

There are various methods of planting, with most depending on a variety of combined conditions such as the length and symmetry of the setts, overhead cables, or trees etc. We can start by examining two fairly straightforward examples:

1) This particular site is a broad ditch of approximately 5 to 6 yards wide. It is several hundred yards long and accommodates a gentle sloping bank in to the waterline.

Where do I start, and how many setts can I consider for planting within the 200-yard length? The simple answer is a safe formula that I have devised. Each sett must be 10 yards apart from one another; therefore the total length of the ditch will accommodate 20 setts. What about the planting depth of each sett? The rule of thumb is generally between 2 feet to 2 feet and 6 inches deep, depending on the overall length of the sett. Setts come in differing denominations of either 3 or 4

Fig. 24 Ditch for planting

lengths. This combination is derived from multiples of 28 inches, which is the length of the 'round' resulting from the mature tree we cut. If a sett is a 3-length tree, planting depth must be 2 feet, alternatively, 2 feet and 6 inches if it is a 4-length tree.

How then, is this done? With the help of an iron rod of approximately 5 feet in length (Fig. 25). One method of achieving this is to take a length of scaffold pole (which is hollow), and insert a piece of iron bar into one end. This must be welded firmly into position, so that a point can be made at the end of the rod by either filing or machining it to a sharp point. This will enable the 'spearing' of the soil to create the necessary depth of hole for planting the sett.

Fig. 25 Doug Watling with Sett Bar

Now we're getting there. We have the setts and we have the means to plant them. From here on we'll continue in the singular.

We need to establish the precise position of where, on the bank, the sett is going to be planted. I would advise the following criteria:

1) What is the direction of the prevailing wind?
2) The depth of the bank itself.
3) How deep is the ditch itself?
4) How adjacent is any cultured land, to the ditch?

Fig. 26 Where on the bank for planting?

These are important considerations and, having assessed the potential impact of each of the above, we need to bear the following in mind:

The *Caerulea's* root structure is shallow, spreading out between 6–8 feet like a giant table underneath the tree. A strongly gusting wind can, in certain circumstances, topple the tree, exposing a great circle of roots lifted out of the ground. If the tree is cut away from the bottom, the root structure, bulky in its own mass, would drop back into its original position, disguising its previously turbulent conduct.

You can now see why the position of where the tree is planted on a sloping bank, is given special consideration. If the tree is positioned too far down towards the water, this would undermine the stability of the tree on the waterside. Alternatively, should you plant high up the bank, your tree may have greater stability but the shade factor, not to mention the root factor, will encroach upon the fertility of crops growing adjacent.

Nevertheless, one must weigh up all the factors discussed and arrive at a final decision as to where planting must occur, if at all, in the scenario discussed above.

Having said that, there may be sufficient space to plant on both sides of the ditch, but remember the shortest distance between the trees thus planted should not be less than 8 yards, so a stagger system is a must. I have noticed that although the 'sail' factor is increased, there is also the question of 'safety in numbers' and an increase in your profit ratio!

We have discussed some eventualities above, but it is now time to start planting.

Plunge the iron bar to the depth required and you will find the deeper you go, the bigger the top of the hole becomes. There is a reason and purpose for this as you will soon find out.

Having chopped a point on the sett, a thumbnail mark being sufficient to note the depth on it, you must **firmly** push the sett into the bottom of the hole (Fig. 27). You must ensure that the point of the sett does indeed get to its full depth and that its path is not hindered by some obstacle. Reaching the thumbnail mark on the sett ensures that the proper planting depth has been reached.

Fig. 27 Planting depth mark

Once the sett is standing in its designated hole, it is imperative to strengthen its upright position by moving the surrounding earth towards the hole and filling it meticulously around the sett. Simply filling the top loosely will leave a vacuum below the surface just where the sett needs to try and form roots to reach nourishment for growth. You must take your sett bar and plunge it repeatedly all around the

Fig. 28 Guarded Sett

Fig. 29 Spring buds

sett, always ensuring you are 4 to 5 inches away from the sett, pitching to a depth of about a foot below the ground. This process will have shaken up the soil around the sett, and leaves you to finally 'heel-in' by systematically stamping the soil 'til the sett is standing firmly upright. It will not now flap about, which would result in the sett's eventual death through lack of nourishment.

One other thing to do now. Remember the rabbits and hares we discussed in the last chapter? – you need to place a spiral rabbit guard around the foot of the sett (Fig. 28).

Also, **do not forget** to come back about twice a year to rub off the shoots that will normally sprout from the entire length of the sett in the spring and through late summer. The easiest way is to reach as high as possible up the sett, **circling it with the hand**, then sweeping the encircling hand down the entire length of the sett rubbing off the buds as you go. You will note that I say BUDS. Don't leave the buds to a point where they become shoots, because you will have to cut these off which in turn will leave knots. We don't make cricket bats with knots in them! (Figs 29, 30, 31 & 32).

2) Let us now consider planting in PLANTATION FORM.

The area utilised for this method must be fairly large, some 3 or 4 acres for example. Make certain that a tractor or other large vehicle can manoeuvre around the field without knocking into and damaging your newly planted trees. They don't take kindly to being knocked about and neither, since we are on the subject, do they take kindly to most of the crop sprays, so have a care if you are considering a secondary crop of hay or light root crops.

Fig. 30 'Circling with hand'

Fig. 31 'Pushing single bud off with hand'

Fig. 32 The effects of bad pruning

The main distinction between planting adjacent to a brook and in a larger plantation is that the rule of planting 8 yards apart no longer applies. The planting distance now becomes 10 yards apart. The reason for doing this is that planting trees in such a large formation leads to overcrowding and often results in trees on the outside growing at a much faster pace than those in the middle. Giving them a little more room

Fig. 33 Plantation form showing access space

Fig. 34 Keeping plantation free of undergrowth

tends to lessen the problem (Fig. 33). You must also keep the area around the bottom of the tree clear of weeds, so as to keep a clean bole and also prevent insects from invading the recesses of the bark causing defects in the resultant timber. (See Chapter 6 for more on this topic.)

The principle of staking setts sometimes arises, but I personally do not recommend it. If the setts originally stood unaided in the sett bed, I see no reason to change the system when planted out. Staking involves supporting a sett by securing a 'tie' about 5 feet up the sett to an adjoining post which, when the wind blows, will quite badly chafe the bark off the sett. This in turn will damage the wood at that point so that it becomes unusable for making Cricket Bats.

All of the conditions that applied to single line planting apply equally to plantation planting, i.e. keeping the shoots off, keeping the weeds down around the bole and **not** spraying weeds but cutting them with a reap hook or similar.

Never, but **NEVER, nail fences to willow trees**. It costs you bats and plays havoc with chain saws (Fig. 36).

Fig. 35 Example of unkempt site

Fig. 36 Damage caused by attached fencing

A knock with a tractor or other machinery, either self-driven or drawn by other means, can destroy up to half of the tree and in some cases kills it entirely. Always plant in straight lines, 10 yards apart both ways. There is little that gives me more pleasure than a properly planted field of Cricket Bat Willow, in the warm sunshine of summer, in full leaf and majestically swaying in the breeze . . . **a truly magnificent sight!** (Fig. 37).

Fig. 37 Perfect example of well kept site. Major Capel-Cure, Blake Hall, Ongar, Essex

A word at this point about guarding the tree. These can be either the rabbit guards or the more extensive type of guards which circle the tree entirely.

The rabbit guard, which we have discussed briefly before, comes in a spiral plastic type, either in a 2 ft or 2 ft and 6 inch version. You may ask what the difference is apart from the obvious one of length; it is in the function of each one. I have used the 2 ft version on many thousands of setts, but believe me that size is useless when seeking to stop "Johnny Hare", the rabbit's larger erstwhile cousin! With his long hind legs, he just stands up and **chews all the bark off above the 2 ft line!** This ruins the sett altogether, since to remove the bark is to kill the tree, for the tree grows from the bark (Fig. 38).

Fig. 38 Sett 'chewed' by hare

So you see, if you have a multiplicity of hares you must use the 2 ft 6 ins guards or even the Netlon plastic lattice type guard available in 3 ft up to 6 ft lengths. Remember, this latter type of guard must always be placed on the sett prior to planting.

A further type of guard is the tubular full-length guard. I am not altogether happy with these in that they cloak the sett from receiving the natural light, causing a canker on the bark giving rise to distorted growth (Fig. 39).

Fig. 39 Tubular full length guard

Finally, if you have the space together with grazing horses and cattle, here is a further alternative. Sink **four stout posts** in a somewhat spacious square round the sett and surround it with **four strands of barbed wire**. Bear in mind in

Fig. 40 Cattle/horse guard

deciding just how big the square should be, a horse has a neck reach of some 4 to 5 feet – hence the statement 'spacious' (Fig. 40). This creates an excellent fence, until it is time to fell the tree. The strength of this fence can be felt whenever I have sought to remove the staples from the fence and felt the barbs of the wire, taking upwards of 30 minutes. As for the stakes, attempting to lift them out of the ground is another story altogether.

One last retrospective thought. Whilst thinking about what you are doing ground wise, always remember to look UP as well. There may be wires, telephone and /or power, there may also be overhanging trees. The willow tree hates to be under any kind of obstacle, be it another tree or anything else which would hinder its growth. Also unhappy in any such case might be the telephone and power authorities, wary that trees might hinder their equipment.

CHAPTER THREE

Where to Plant

During the course of my regular visits around the counties and estates of England, I am constantly perusing the possibilities of starting new willow plantations. The question which usually follows 'Whether' to plant is, 'Where' and 'Is the land suitable?'

The latter question is always a prerequisite, because unlike some generic species of willow, which can grow in any type of soil, the *Salix Alba Caerulea* demands a specific soil type and condition in which to thrive and produce high quality white wood.

I can quote a reverse example of the above to illustrate an opposing scenario, when growing conditions are not quite ideal. There are many sites in the Suffolk outback which are well known for their timber growing prowess, but which I know will never produce what I would classify as top quality Cricket Bat Willow. An example in question is a site near Bury St Edmunds which grows hundreds of willow trees but has, to date, never produced any willow above a Grade 3 quality. The reasons are visibly apparent to an expert willow grower (Fig. 41).

Fig. 41 Example of an unsuitable site for growing Cricket Bat Willow

The area is an over soggy mass of peat, saturated and stagnated, totally unsuitable for growing Cricket Bat Willow. It would seem that someone took the old saying "If you've got a bit of wet land, plant willow on it" literally, with the consequences that all the land yields is what we call 'common wood'. I will discuss 'common wood' at some length in a later chapter.

There are occasions when decisions concerning "whether" and "where" to plant are influenced by circumstances beyond one's control.

In 1993, I had the great privilege of meeting and speaking with His Royal Highness, the Duke of Edinburgh. During the course of watching a cricket match, I raised the question with His Royal Highness of the possibility of growing Cricket Bat Willow within Windsor Great Park, a world-renowned area of Crown Estate.

His Royal Highness, after a lengthy thoughtful pause, turned to me and inquired "Would it grow in this area?" I promptly confirmed that some fine specimens were felled adjacent to the River Thames near a sewage works at Old Windsor. The Duke, displaying an exemplary timing of wit and repartee, exclaimed "Oh dear, I didn't know we grew 'aromatic' willow trees!" Notwithstanding, he promised I should meet with his Head Ranger to arrange an inspection. This I did, and made the journey to Windsor to meet with the gentleman in question.

I have visited Windsor on several occasions on the invitation of the Australian 'Crusaders' Cricket Team and their manager, the larger than life and hugely charismatic Swan Richards (a pillar of strength in promotional cricket, both in Australia and in England) (Fig. 42).

Fig. 42 Swan Richards with Author's wife

I had personally felt that the sight of willow trees would add to the scenery around the cricket pitch and grow particularly well.

At my recommendation, the Head Ranger gasped in polite expostulation, throwing up his hands, "Heavens no" he said, in a mode of animated explanation, "the powers that be would be quite horrified". This said, he led me to a part of the Great Park which I found to be totally unsuitable, as it was arid and stony. "You win some, you lose some" he remarked. Our patient searching was soon rewarded, as I found a suitable area that fulfilled the Crown Estate's criteria as well. Over 70 trees were planted in 1994.

I have stressed previously, and will continue to do so in the remainder of this book, that an ideal growing site is one which is in a valley, lowland as opposed to upland, with a river or stream running through fields, where soil breaks down to a fine tilth. Another important caveat is to avoid acidic, stony or arid soil, including that which harbours blue clay. This is an important cautionary tale, which I shall elaborate fully in Chapter 6.

To revert back to the issue of suitability of growing site, I recall one instance when I was asked to pass judgement on a site on the outskirts of Colchester, by a client in a telephone request. Essex, being my county of residence, is well known to me, and having decided to agree with my client's request in principle, a thought rushed through my head. I decided to inspect the site first hand before concurring with his wishes.

Upon arrival at the site, accompanied by my host, my first impressions were that the site had all the hallmarks of a promising willow growing area. A straight, long ditch, almost a mile in length, in the midst of a lush valley. With great anticipation, I pulled on my trusted 'wellies', and marched forward in a businesslike manner. I walked on the stubbled field adjacent to the planting area . . . As I made my way towards the brook, totally unaware of what was about to befall me, I suddenly found myself sinking into a muddy quagmire, and before I could look at my boots, I was being sucked downwards into this watery quicksand. In double quick time, I had sunk knee deep, rescued at the last moment by my host. The air was pervaded with an almighty dose of obnoxious stench! The stench of pig! "How long have you kept pigs in the area?" I enquired. "Oh . . . years" he waved with a dismissive movement of his hand. "Used to keep 'em penned at the top end near the brook, but they blocked up the ditch with their effluent and it kept flooding the field down 'ere, so I thought we'd plant willows and dry the land out a bit".

Let me state quite unequivocally . . . *Salix Alba Caerulea* and pigs **DO NOT** mix. Pigs can, and usually do, render a row of trees worthless in a period of approximately six months. Whereas pigs and their effluent are the *nemesis* for willow trees, chickens on the other hand can have a positively beneficial effect on willow trees – in a strange way!

In numerous instances, some of the finest willow I have seen, and the quickest growing, have emerged from an area of 'chicken runs'. In a perverse manner, chicken feed contains powerful fertilisers which distributed as natural chicken manure in copious doses, can act as a positive catalyst to a willow tree. The excessive use of chicken manure, however, can overpower growth in a willow tree and will burn the roots, eventually killing the tree.

The question of suitability of sites, is best broached with common sense, and farmers that I have met in my lifetime seem to be rich in this commodity, more so than any other type of person that I have met in any other walk of life.

Take this farming tale. Farmer Harry Metson and a visiting urban friend, set off with a tractor and trailer to bring back a load of hay from a neighbouring village where Harry Metson owns a large meadow beyond the railway bridge.

They spent the entire morning piling bale after bale onto Harry's trailer, when the urban friend, noticing the increasingly precarious position of the bales, remarked, "Isn't that rather high Harry?" "No" said Harry quickly. "I'd like to get all we've got left in this meadow on one last load". Harry and his friend pursued their task with relentless vigour, until the trailer was carrying a tower of hay bales. Having collected all the bales, Harry and his friend trundled unsteadily out of the field and up the road to the railway bridge where, without seeming to happen, a crowd built up. On witnessing this extraordinary trailer, they started exchanging unkind comments about the state of the towering bales of hay.

Harry's friend, by now sensing the embarrassment of such an enterprise, joined rank with the onlookers and passed on some of his views to Harry. "I told you it was too high Harry, NOW we're in a right muddle" he remarked looking concerned. Harry nonchalantly jumped off the tractor, went round to each of the trailer wheels, and routinely, let out half the air from each tyre. When he had finished, Harry casually jumped back onto the tractor, and chugged the large 'monument' of hay skilfully through the tunnel under the bridge, and out towards a garage approximately 100 yards up the road. All this time the inquisitive crowd, together with his visitor, sauntered behind the tractor and trailer, their remarks becoming more sarcastic with every yard of progress. Harry, on reaching the garage, pulled up and inflated each trailer tyre with the maximum air permitted, and turned to his urban friend, "Well, are you coming then?" His urban friend was flabbergasted. Harry turned to the crowd and tapped his own forehead, exclaiming "Common sense" he chuckled shrewdly, "that's what you want, mate!" and drove off with a smile on his face.

Heed the following and never forget. . . .

Always choose a moist, but not wet, well tilled, soft loamy soil. In the case of a ditch or a stream, be sure:

1. It runs consistently all year.
2. It is not subject to pollution from manure or effluent, and that includes "rust" (it turns the tree blue).
3. Do not plant under any overhead cables, i.e. power or telephone.
4. Avoid letting roaming cattle, sheep or horses, enter the planted area.
5. Keep away from the tree when ploughing so as not to risk damaging the root system.

6. Beware of drains (I have seen a willow root worm its way 30 yards up a drain!)
7. Do not, when trimming hedges, use the willow tree as a parking place for the hook, blade first.
8. Lastly, willow loves running water, therefore, always plant on low ground, you won't find running water on top of a hill.

Remember this . . . look after them and they will look after you – I promise.

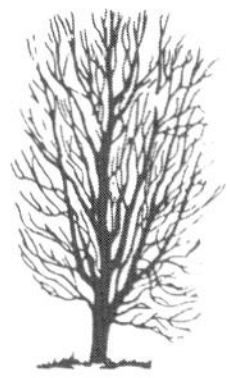

CHAPTER 4

Grown as a Crop – Not Forestry as such

The subject of Licences in relation to the felling of a specific crop has and always will remain a contentious and an idiosyncratic piece of bureaucratic nuisance to me. My late Father, were he alive today, might have treated the whole affair as reason for *Armageddon*. How on earth can a legislative body be so insensitive and ignorant in drafting a piece of legislation affecting the willow grower, which does not manifest the requirements of the willow industry, within it? It is in a sense akin to expecting a farmer conducting his normal business of growing crops, and in the same breath ordering him against the harvest of the very same crops. Many apt words come to mind which sum up the issue of Felling Licences, but 'bureaucratic nonsense' seems to top the bill.

The Forestry Commission seems intent in keeping an all-embracing set of conditions within the legislation that seems too generic for the specific requirements of willow growing. Yet at the same time they seem to disregard the willow grower's standpoint. "Who are we to have a say?" they keep asking. We have after all been in the business for at least four generations.

Why the willow trade has not been treated as a special exception remains a sore subject. Willow is specifically grown for felling, and cannot be simply construed as part of a larger environmental issue. The willow trade is highly specialised and dedicated solely to the planting, growing and felling of willows. Our industry is not about a bunch of cowboys rushing around like some bounty hunters looking to fell trees in an arbitrary manner. The authorities are aware that willow trees are felled, but that at the same time, many are planted for future growth, thereby replenishing with new plants at the same time. As I have suggested in previous chapters, we are always seeking to grow more and more new plantations, so that a natural equilibrium between felling and growing can be maintained. We are the lifeblood of cricket bat making, and clearly without us the cricket bat industry would be dead. No one else knows, and practices the science of propagating willow trees more than we do.

In recent times though, there has been a constant dialogue between the Forestry Commission and ourselves regarding the lead-time required before we can commence felling any particular tree. They have realised that their previous directives which embraced all manner of trees, do not apply to the willow tree specifically, and that to us 'time is of the essence'. At certain points in the season, we cannot wait for 3 months or even a mere 3 weeks, and the Forestry Commission's standpoint is even more bewildering, when eventually they have to concur with our requests.

I have been lucky in that around our own areas of Essex, Suffolk and Norfolk we have enjoyed a good rapport with the Forestry Authority, and they do go to extraordinary lengths to help us, in our times of need. Pat Mitchell, now retired, has been a pillar of support during his time with the Forestry Commission. Mark Pritchard of Cambridge is currently directly responsible for Cricket Bat Willow, and we owe him a debt of gratitude in relation to his support on the subject of felling licences.

There are enormous commercial pressures placed upon us to fulfil demand for Cricket Bat Willow, not only from within the United Kingdom, but from all parts of the world. This means that bat makers in different parts of the world have their own seasons and schedules to adhere to according to their particular market. We are therefore constantly, throughout the year, rain or shine, winter or summer, always striving to meet the requirements of bat makers – correct grades of willow in sufficient numbers and of course at the right price. Delays, however caused, mean higher costs, and ultimately loss of our business credibility.

Our business of Cricket Bat Willow must therefore, never be included in or treated as a general forestry issue; ours is a specialised business, deserving of individual treatment on its own merit. I remember one instance when I met with a Forestry Commission official in an attempt to clarify our standpoint. On arrival at the site where our trees were situated, he quickly glanced around and in typically condescending official manner quipped, "Now then, Mr Watling, where are your 'stands' of willow?" Let me explain, by 'stands', he was referring to stands of other types of wood that he had been more used to seeing such as Fir, Larch, Ash etc., which can be commonly found in large numbers around Thetford and various parts of Suffolk. It seems that this was his first encounter with Cricket Bat Willow, and ours are predominantly singular and grow by sides of fields, rivers and brooks.

"Well, there's one right behind you" I said, pointing to a large willow tree behind him. Looking perplexed, and irritated he replied, "Come, come Mr Watling, I didn't come all this way to be made to look like a fool – where are the willow 'stands'?" I took him by the arm, pointing the way and said to him, "This tree is one of them". He looked confused, and after a thoughtful pause said, ". . . So, *that's* a willow tree, is it?" I am not at liberty to print the contents of the thoughts that rushed through my mind at that point; I will merely leave it to your imagination! This then, was a meeting with an official of the Forestry Commission to discuss the granting of a licence to fell willow trees, and what you have seen described was the sum total of his expertise on a subject that he was expected to pass 'judgement' upon. The plain truth is that he did not know and indeed could not tell what a willow tree was when he saw one!!!

After I had given the official a crash course in Cricket Bat Willow, his whole mood changed. "Mr Watling" he said, a warm smile dissolving his bureaucratic attitude, "I am indebted to you more than I can say". He shook my hand vigorously in gratitude, when rather puzzled at his sudden about turn I asked him, "Why are you so profuse in your thanks?" Sounding gleefully confident, he replied, "It will give me immense pleasure to go back to the office and regale all the information you have imparted to me – so I shall feel superior for weeks to come". At this point, armed with his newly acquired knowledge, and a smug look of self-satisfaction, he drove off.

I feel strongly that a powerful body consisting of Cricket Bat Willow suppliers and specialists, should unite their views on the matter of licences, and lobby the Minister of Agriculture, so that we can emancipate our trade from the restrictive legislation which wrongfully includes our specialised trade as part of a general wood felling industry, which it clearly is not. I am often reminded of a statement made by the former Prime Minister, The Right Honourable John Major, when he said, "We must free our industry of bureaucratic restrictions and red tape." I am adamant that such an example is absolutely vital for our specialised industry of Cricket Bat Willow. All we are interested in is furthering and developing our specialised industry and not contravening legislation applicable to other types of wood.

One last word on the matter. At times we say, "Leave it to the Professionals". This caveat has become a hallmark of our business, and we survive and are judged daily by the high standards that we set in our work. Then, we should continue and be allowed to pursue with diligence the time honoured and nurtured skills of growing Cricket Bat Willow, passed down through time immemorial by our forefathers, without bureaucratic impediments placed in our path.

CHAPTER 5

Harvesting the Crop

"When is the right time to fell a Cricket Bat Willow tree?" That's a little like "How long is a piece of string?" I will discuss some of the reasons which determine timing of harvest in Chapter 6, when dealing with 'Diseases and Defects' but, for the time being, I have devoted this chapter to the process of 'Harvesting the Crop'.

Do not be surprised if I tell you that of 100 trees planted at the same time, not all may be ready for felling in the first cutting, and that it may not be possible to fell even the selected ones in the sequence that one desires.

As I have explained in the earlier chapters of this book, there are variations in how and where willow trees are planted. The extent to which growth rate is achieved is influenced by the position of the tree, the condition and type of soil it is standing in, not to mention how the winds and rain have treated it over its 15–16 years of growth. Also, has it been watered during times of famine, i.e. those long hot months when summer heat has been excessive. Let us not discount the influence of animals. Cattle and horses, who develop a taste for the outer bark as an alternative to their natural feed, can subject a willow to a life of poor growth (Fig. 43).

Fig. 43 Cattle/horse damaged tree resulting in poor growth

There are, of course, multifarious reasons leading to differing rates of growth, which I will discuss in due course.

Assuming all the correct growing criteria have been satisfied, how then should a tree look ? These are some of the questions one would normally pose:

Fig. 44 Close-up of perfect bark specimen

Fig. 45 Measuring prime timber prior to felling

Fig. 46 Perfectly grown timber i.e. pure white

1. Is it straight ?
2. Is it top full and round ?
3. Does the bark look clean, without signs of blemish ?
4. Examine in between the bark breaks. Can you see the clean light tan colour which can only come from clean strong growth? (Fig. 44)
5. Does the tree trunk measure between 56 and 60 inches in circumference at chest height, on a tree aged between 15 and 16 years old ? (Fig. 45)

A close comparison to our photographs should bear a good resemblance, if the answer is 'yes' to the above questions. In such a case you have before you a fine top grade tree of value – how much? Show it to me and I will guarantee you will be pleased.

In the course of my travels, either lecturing throughout the world, or in pursuit of fine timber, I am still surprised to see trees grown in unsuitable sites. But when you do find 'crème de la crème' then I share my late Father's sentiments when I see one (Fig. 47).

Fig. 47 'Crème de la Crème' (whole tree)

He would take one look at a prime example and start examining the tree, slowly walking around it, in deep appreciation and totally mesmerised by its beauty. "Ahh . . . Mm . . . a beautiful tree . . . a marvellous piece of timber . . . just look at that growth . . . feel the soft, smooth bark", he would say. He'd stand with a hand on both sides of the tree and peer upwards into a perfectly crowned top and then, coming down the trunk with his eyes, would conduct a process of quick fire mental arithmetic rapidly calculating the number of clefts and grades of willow it would produce, all in a short space of time. He would then turn to me and say, "Look at that, son – drink it in, that's class that is . . . Now tell me, how many best bats can you get out of that tree?" To my amazement, he would always be within an accuracy of one or two . . . and that would be because of 'awkward splits' that might occur when the tree was opened up (Fig. 48).

Fig. 48 'Awkward splits'

Fig. 49 Damage marks

Let me explain further. When the tree is cut into cricket bat lengths of 28 inches, as soon as the saw reaches the core you can usually detect an audible 'Tchk', which is the result of air reaching the centre causing the core to split outwards. This can sometimes result in the loss of a bat when finally splitting the round into clefts (Fig. 50).

At the beginning of the chapter I said that it is almost impossible for a 'clear fell' to be effected within a large number of trees growing together because of their proximity and varying rates of growth. In particular, felling is made even more dif-

Fig. 50 'Lost' Cleft

ficult if, having pinpointed a select number of trees, they are required to be felled within the plantation. One has to ensure that sufficient precautions are taken to avoid contact between the falling tree and those close to it. It is purely this proximity which sometimes causes 'brushing' rather than incompetence on the part of the tree feller.

Yes, I am aware that it is possible to send a man up and 'top' the tree, or parts of the tree, so that it will fell without brushing another tree, but in the main very little actual damage is done. Usually ten minutes suffices to trim a few pieces off the 'brushed' top, without future detriment since the tree would be within future felling plans anyway.

Overhead power lines and telephone cables can, however, provide difficulties in tight places, sometimes resulting in a call-out of the necessary authorities. Believe it or not, such a call is really appreciated, because to take down a couple of wires means far less time and effort when pre-planned, rather than being faced with clearing up and renewing lines knocked down, not to mention the cost of possible damage occasioned (Fig. 51). All this could have been avoided if the person planting the area in the first had remembered to '**look up**' when assessing the suitability of the site. (See Chapter Two.)

It is, of course, a 'must' to remember to replant in 'due season' where felling has taken place so that future supplies of Cricket Bat Willow will not be jeopardised.

Frankly this does not present a problem for us. In order to school our customers in the practice of planting, we have devised a process where we freely supply setts

Fig. 51 Power wires

in season for 'one on one' system, guaranteeing the supply and involving the customer in replanting – having thoroughly demonstrated the principle of planting and guarding. This, in our view, develops a personal interest in the subsequent growth of the tree.

A note of caution here, however. There have been occasions where we have returned to purchase the mature tree when the grower has developed such an attachment that he is most reluctant to sell because **he** planted it.

CHAPTER 6

DISEASES AND DEFECTS

I imagine that this chapter will have much more impact than any other within this book.

It is quite easy to extol the virtues of almost anything, but to detract includes one or two things sooner swept under the carpet . . . **NOT** however in this book. I am quite prepared to thoroughly explain or analyse all of my following remarks. The reason for this is that it allows the grower to avoid unnecessary heartache when harvest time arrives. So here goes!

There are two particular diseases of a bacteriological nature that are 'killers'. Having made that bold statement let me hasten to assure you that I should have concluded '. . . but only if you let them'.

The first is commonly known as *Honey Fungus* or *Bark Disease*. Its correct term is "*Armillariella Mellea*" (Fig. 52). This condition displays various symptoms, amongst those that become commonly visible are some of the following.

The tree is usually in its early years – say, up to 10 years. The top will begin to look thin and the leaves will pale almost to a creamy yellow in colour and eventually, of course, drop, leaving a gaunt skeleton.

The bark around the bottom of the tree will split off and crack open leaving a "whitey" dead scum of the bacteria which has killed by cutting off the life blood of the tree – **the sap**.

Fig. 52 "Armillariella Mellea"

Figs. 53 & 54 "Armillariella Mellea" showing white scum

Beware and be warned, this very potent disease can travel to the adjacent tree or trees in a very short space of time and, if left, can destroy the entire area as the spore increases.

This scourge almost became an epidemic in the 1994/95 summer which brought the very hot and very dry conditions that cause "*Armillariella Mellea*" to thrive. I had occasion to warn the members of the U.E.A. Watermark Disease Committee (of which I am a member) that the disease was prevalent, since some members were attributing the disease to lack of water. Indeed a lot of the success of its increase is largely due to a lack of knowledge as to just what it really was, although if one used the more widely known term of '*Honey Fungus*' there was instant apprehension and recognition amongst willow growers.

I have referred in previous chapters to the importance of invoking 'common sense' and 'good husbandry' in this or any other farming predicament. The same caveat applies when one is combating this killer disease. Something resembling a 'scorched earth' approach is required, and swiftly at that. You need to cut down the sick tree at once, and burn everything on the stump, thereby having the effect of 'cauterising' the whole area thus preventing further breeding of the bacteria.

There are some in the fraternity who refuse to heed the serious nature of the disease and avoid swift, thorough remedial action. They do so at their own peril.

Early in 1994, I visited a friend of mine and to my horror I noticed a tree in a plantation which had collapsed and died on its stump, riddled with the killer disease. I vehemently stressed to him the importance of eradicating the disease swiftly (by employing the method that I have outlined previously) in order to prevent further spread of the disease. He laughed and said I was being much too particular and that it wouldn't hurt to stay there. In fact he rather liked to see the contrast with the sound trees around it.

In early 1995, I had occasion to visit the same estate, this time with the owner. He, in vivid contrast to my friend who in the previous year had waved away my cautionary words, saw instantly what I was trying to do. On seeing the state of the diseased tree he ordered its immediate destruction, together with two others nearby to which the disease had spread during the intervening year.

I cannot stress strongly enough the need to undertake remedial action the moment the first dreaded signs appear. Let us remind ourselves of the very important steps required to pre-empt the onset of an epidemic:

1. Fell the diseased tree.
2. Cut into manageable pieces.
3. Douse the stump with old engine oil and burn **everything** you have cut on the stump.

FINALLY,

4. ***DO NOT*** replant in the immediate vicinity for at least **five years**.

Another lethal killer disease is the "*Erwinia Salicis*". This has been prevalent for 45 years or so, and once more its spread can be attributed to the fact that very few people were aware of the nature of the symptoms (Fig. 55).

Fig. 55 Early "Erwinia Salicis"

Mainly because a lot of people had difficulty with pronouncing the Latin name "*Erwinia Salicis*", in the early years it was commonly referred to as "The Watermark Disease". This is the title by which it is still known today.

Research into the various aspects of the Watermark Disease has been sporadic, but the Lever Hulme Trust and the Thomas Price Trust (Essex) funded a series of 3-year projects which were carried out at the University of Leeds in the early 1980's with a view to eradicating the disease.

This research, by its very nature, is a long-term process. In April 1989 it was moved to the University of East Anglia at Norwich in the School of

Biological Sciences headed by Dr. John G. Turner.

Clearly, such research requires funding, and this has been made possible by the voluntary levy raised by those involved in the Cricket Bat Industry. In March 1989 the Watermark Disease Control Group was formed comprising various members of the industry, covering Willow Merchants, some Willow growing farmers and Bat Manufacturers, as follows:

WILLOW MERCHANTS

- Anglian Willow Service of High Ongar, Essex (ourselves)
- J.S.Wright & Sons Ltd of Great Leighs, Essex
- Edgar Watts Ltd of Bungay, Suffolk
- H.J.R. Foskett of Bromwell, Suffolk (formerly George Green)

WILLOW GROWING FARMERS

- Robert Brice of Witham, Essex
- Paul Buxton of Chipping Ongar, Essex
- David J.M. Daniels of Sudbury, Suffolk
- Strutt & Parker of Ipswich, Suffolk
- Bernie Facer of Huntingdon, Cambridgeshire
- P.A. Grove-White of Wormingford, Essex
- J. Minter of Boxted, Essex
- G.H. Thoroughgood of Southminster, Essex
- R. Yates of Brampton, Suffolk

BAT MANUFACTURERS

- Gray Nicolls of Robertsbridge, East Sussex
- Hunts County Bats of Huntingdon, Cambridgeshire
- Stuart Surridge & Co. Ltd of Witham, Essex
- Gunn & Moore Ltd of Nottingham

At that first meeting, the Essex County Council was represented by Mr. Michael Wortley of the Estates Department. Also present were The Dean, Professor D.R. Davies, and Dr. John G. Turner of the University of East Anglia jointly heading the research team. Continuity was provided by Mr. T.R. Preece of the University of Leeds, together with Dr. & Mrs Sims of the Thomas Phillips Price Trust (Essex). The Forestry Commission also gave support to the project and were represented by Mr. B. Greig and Mr. K. Stott, later to be joined by Dr. J. Gibbs. Over the years, certain changes were made due to circumstances.

The group was competently Chaired under the auspices of Mr. Robert Brice (Chairman of the County Landowners Association), alas now deceased.

Indeed as you can see from the credentials, we have a highly knowledgeable cross-section of bodies whose sole interest lies in the welfare of Cricket Bat Willow.

Let us then identify the monster in our midst which threatens the Cricket Bat Willow. How can we tell if it is under threat?

Take this scenario. It is a hot day in the middle of Summer. The sky is blue, with a light breeze gently ruffling the lush green leaves of a row, or plantation, of Cricket Bat Willow trees. You stop to admire the growth of your crop, when suddenly your eye catches sight of an area of reddy – brown dead leaves in the top of one or possibly more trees, contrasting starkly against the lush green leaf background. You should at this point put all systems red alert! (Fig. 56)

Fig. 56 Dead leaves in top – Watermark Disease

Fig. 57 Felled diseased tree

Your attitude should be the same as if you had been told the 'plague' had struck – because that is how extremely urgent it is to treat this discovery and to act **immediately**.

Action is basically the same as for "*Armillariella Mellea*". Fell at once and burn on the stump to prevent spread and to cauterise the area of possible future spread.

How then does the disease spread? There are conflicting schools of thought on this issue, but I can offer a definitively authoritative opinion on this subject, as I have dealt with it on a regular basis over 45 years of my life. There are basically two principle modes that aid the spread of the disease . . .

The first, is that the disease uses the root system of the tree as a convenient conduit, spreading either through land or more commonly through water from infected trees nearby.

The second, is that it is spread by a process similar to seed propagation, by 'injection' into the top of a healthy tree. When the disease is firmly established, small weeping 'bluey purple' coloured eruptions mark the smooth green bark, as well as in

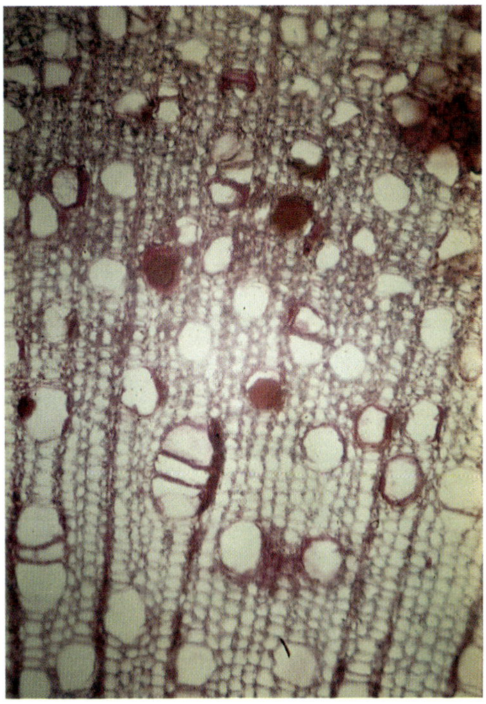

Fig. 58 Bacteria cells

crevices where a branch joins the main tree. These eruptions ooze a sticky fluid which attracts insects, who then become prey for birds, such as blackbird, thrush and starling. The birds, whilst eating insects in the infected area, become carriers of the killer disease in the form of bacteria picked up on their beaks. This is then transmitted, during the process of pecking on a healthy tree, by injecting the bacteria into the bark.

Quite logical isn't it? But then after 4 generations of experience one would expect to know that kind of thing, unlike the scientists who will only accept it when it is scientifically proven – as it now has been.

Fig. 59 Bluey-purple colour – clear evidence of the prescence of "Erwinia Salicis"

Our Dr. John Turner has made strides in the identification of the disease and areas in which it thrives, and is currently experimenting with various culches in an effort to produce disease resistant Cricket Bat Willow plants (Fig. 60).

Fig. 60 Various culches

I wish Dr. Turner well in pursuit of this elusive strain, but I remain entirely unconvinced of his possible success in this area. Why? – Let us explore the theory.

The *modus operandie* appears to be to create some kind of 'pedigree' by breeding out all possible defects that could attract disease in the first place, and whilst I can agree in principle, ordinary common practice confounds that principle.

Certain species of willow can, and will, thrive in terrible conditions (i.e. bad soil, poor drainage, excessive moisture in the soil, bad positioning, etc), where anything of a 'High Bred' nature will succumb at the first attack, however weak. Now apply my 'source of attack by direct injection' and you can see, at once, the experiment is doomed to failure.

The answer, which has a proven track record, is the simple method of good husbandry, together with the innate understanding of the elements that shape growth in a willow tree. The mastery of all these prerequisites is, I regret, only achieved through bitter first hand experience. Hence I believe, with good sound advice, early planning and swift remedial action, you can be successful in growing the Cricket Bat Willow.

I prescribe the good old-fashioned method of dousing the diseased stump with old engine oil and burning on the stump. There is no better method of attacking the 'enemy' than this. I am always concerned at the apparent apathy displayed by the farmer who decides that he simply does not have the time to cut down the tree and burn it when the disease strikes. The result is that when the Disease Inspectors eventually arrive, the damage has been done. Whole areas are putrefied and spreading the disease by the hour. Six months is all that's needed to infect 20 trees from one infection.

From the first time this dreaded scourge came to our notice we adopted the scorched earth policy and found it has paid off handsomely for all our customers who have heeded our advice.

Also in the earlier years, the disease was propagated by taking Sett Stakes (See Chapter One) from already diseased trees and thereby spreading the disease through already infected stock.

Enough then about "*Erwinia Salicis*". Let us cover some of the lesser infections that occur in the Cricket Bat Willow.

'**Speck**' is one such defect. It is a particular nuisance and is found in boggy areas and less suitable sites where farmers sometimes plant because they don't know what else to grow there, and are loathe to take advice on the subject.

In short, "the devil in the woodpile", to coin a phrase, is a tiny insect which takes up residence in lush undergrowth – particularly that which is allowed to accumulate around the bottom of growing trees. These insects gradually penetrate into the cambium, or inner bark, and happily breed. Both they and their offspring leave the evidence of their being, in the shape of small black 'specks', which totally ruin what may have been a pure white bat face and reduce it to a common quality piece of wood which is far inferior in both quality and price!

Fig. 61 Speck in Willow

How can we successfully tackle '**Speck**'?

1) I have mentioned the importance of clearing the undergrowth around the butt or bole of the tree, thereby denying the insects the luxury of a convenient breeding ground.
2) Avoid planting willow in such areas. They do not conform to even the minimum standards of land required to grow a Cricket Bat Willow tree successfully.

Certain signs give clues as to the presence of '**Speck**'. The undergrowth, that I have mentioned before, can be quite thick and bushy, consisting of blackthorn or the common sloe. If you were to cut a piece from the stem of the 'sloe' bush you would find it full of the little black specks of which I have spoken (Fig. 61).

Now, let us address another 'detriment'. I'll call it no more than that, but it breaches the saleable aspect of Cricket Bat Willow and is misunderstood. I am referring to '**Butterfly Stain**' or its closely associated '**Tiger Bar Stain**'.

Much is said in cricketing circles about 'stain'. Some call it a defect, others a disease. There is really so much conflicting information in circulation about this subject that I wish to end this debate conclusively, once and for all. 'Stain' is **not** a disease, but merely a symptom of particular growing conditions. In fact certain of the '**Butterfly**' varieties are actually capable of enhancing the performance of the bat.

For all those who wonder and debate aimlessly about the cause of stain, let me make it clear. Stain is caused by the interaction of acidic properties on the root structure of the tree.

What then causes this excess in acidic properties which leads to the onset of stain in a Cricket Bat Willow? Several types of soil, such as those made up of heavy blue clay or those that are riddled with stones or soil that contains common rubbish such as brick rubble. Iron for instance, in quantity, will turn a Cricket Bat Willow **blue**.

The process of staining occurs as a result of the following. The tree and its root structure generally grow outwards, with the main roots throwing out bunches of 'loofah' like suckers which, as they search for water and nourishment under the surface of the ground, are confronted occasionally by areas of stone. This slows down temporarily the rate and direction of growth, consequently checking the flow of sap, which then, interacting with the resultant acidity, creates and causes stainy colouring.

Fig. 62 Butterfly Stain

Fig. 63 Tiger Bar Stain

In the event of the interaction being slight, the resulting stain gives a delicate marking akin to the subtle colours of a King George butterfly. Hence the vaunted term '**Butterfly Stain**' was coined (Fig. 62).

Fig. 64 Bar stain break on bark

When the soil consists primarily of blue clay, then the resultant stain in the willow resembles a '**Tiger**' stripe (Fig. 63).

Furthermore, there is sharper colouring and an opening in the outer bark of the tree, which can render the tree worthless even for making inferior quality cricket bats (Fig. 64).

Finally we need to cover the aspect of damage by sprays. The damage caused by crop spraying has never been properly assessed by the farmer because there is no obvious outward symptom. Only when it is felled can the extent of the damage be seen – which may be anything from five to ten years after the act.

We are caught between the 'devil and the deep blue sea' in that almost any of the sprays currently in use to control insects or diseases, are literally death to newly planted Cricket Bat Willow Setts. Mature trees, on the other hand, whilst showing a bit of leaf dieback at point of contact with spray will disguise any inner damage.

The effect of the spray takes the following path. As the tree grows there is an increase in sap flow. When the crop spray comes to rest on the leaf, it is absorbed into the sap flow, eventually making its way towards inner bark ('cambium') causing the outer bark to separate away from the main tree. There is a temporary respite in growth where this separation occurs, and there is left what is known as a 'deadline'. This indicates a breakdown in growth patterns when viewed after the tree is felled.

Of course, the tree does recover, but only from an external view. The real damage has already been done, and the 'deadline' causes weakness in growth and becomes a point at which the wood can be easily separated. The point is made conclusively by referring to the illustration (Fig. 65).

Fig. 65 Deadline – showing separation of wood

You can see that where the 'deadline' is indicated, the outer part of the tree has detached itself from the main centre. This is directly caused by the effects of crop spray. This diagram illustrates that the tree was probably affected in its 6th year, but then went on to recover. There is a possibility of recovering portions of the tree to make inferior quality bats (note marked cleft). Had this 'deadline' taken hold some 5 years later, then the whole tree would have been rendered a total waste . . . simply firewood.

Fig. 66 Comparison of Speck, Butterfly Stain, Tiger Bar Stain etc.

I therefore stress once again, DO NOT spray pesticides near willow trees. It can be a costly mistake. For example, 20 trees at a unit price of £120/150, is equal to £2,400 worth of firewood.

A slightly less serious ailment is the somewhat colloquially named "bumknot". This ghastly looking protrusion can be found growing towards the bottom end of the trunk, usually beneath heavy undergrowth which is cause of its proliferation (Fig. 69).

The "bumknot", together with another growth defect known as "shees" or "grape", causes marks in the wood, which either downgrades the cleft or renders it unworthy for cricket bat making. Let me explain how this happens (Fig 68).

When the tree is growing, it adds to its own circumference. This causes the outer bark to stretch in order facilitate growth. The tree pushes out little spikes to act as safety valves in order to ease the stretch. These penetrate the 'cambium' and outer bark to allow it to break gently and naturally so that it eases into normal formation.

Fig. 67 Wind damage on cleft

Normally these spikes grow naturally and at a reasonable rate. This rate of growth may vary according to soil composition, whereby the spikes may overgrow and develop their own characteristics (Fig. 71).

Fig. 68 Bumknot

Fig. 69 Bumknot on tree

Fig. 70 'Shees' or 'Grape'

Fig. 71 Bark spikes growing from wood of tree NOT the bark

Fig. 72 Developing in bunches leaving marks in wood which results in visual blemishes on the face of the bat

Where growing conditions are conducive to rapid growth, the "shee" will grow out into a hideous looking protrusion.

It is not so much the outer bulbous growth that causes problems, but the portion that grows inwards into the tree. It is a **brown pith growth** which drives deep in towards the core.

By this time you will be wondering. . . . "What comes next. . . ..?"

NEXT comes the Goat Moth ("*Cossus Cossus*"). A pesky pest if ever there was one. It's rather a large moth which chews a hole through the bark of the tree, usually anywhere from one to two feet from the bottom of the butt, again usually in a root crevice where there is already an accessible entrance where the ground root comes out of the ground and blends into the trunk.

This pest can also make a chamber in the soft cambium under the much harder cover of the outer bark. The moth then ravenously drills a tunnel up to 2 feet long with half an inch diameter. This tunnel becomes home to its larvae of between two and two and a half inches long. The larvae are white underneath with a deep purple colouring on their backs (Figs. 73 & 74).

Be careful, a close encounter with them will cause them to emit a foul smelling

Fig. 73 Goat Moth ('Cossus Cossus')

Fig. 74 Damaged wood caused by Goat Moth

'spit'. Clearly, "*Cossus Cossus*" spell trouble, ensure that you deal with them at the first signs.

Apart from those diseases and pests we have mentioned, we will conclude this chapter with a few common sense factors.

The use of nails and barbed wire on willow trees has been previously mentioned. Other foreign bodies to be added are horseshoes, shrapnel and shotgun pellets (Fig. 75).

Thoughtless cutting of the boughs of the tree should be avoided. Each piece of the top of the tree has a role to perform. Clearly, let it go on and do exactly that.

Fig. 75 Fencing wire/ Discolouration due to foreign bodies i.e. nails and barbed wire

CHAPTER 7

PREPARING THE RAW MATERIAL: SAWING OUT: GRADING

In this chapter of '**The Life and Times of the Cricket Bat Willow**' the logical progression of matters takes us through the inspection, felling, splitting and 'sawing out' of the Willow tree. Additionally, as an added bonus, I would like to take the discussion to the topic of grading, as well.

After having ceaselessly pursued this business over the last five decades, I have built up and retained an exclusively select clientele. This is the culmination of my industry and application, but also of having practised my late Father's words literally in my own business life. He would constantly extol the following virtues, "*Take care of the people you deal with, treat them with honesty, pay them fairly for what you buy, look after a) their property, and b) their fences. The last thing they want is the law calling upon them in the early hours because their cows were all over the surrounding neighbourhood, all because some idiot failed to replace the fences*". I can honestly confirm that since I took over the reins from my Father all those years ago, we have been constantly commended for the diligence with which we pursue the business of mending willow growers' fences. In fact on several occasions our replacements have been better than the originals.

Our credentials have been painstakingly achieved through the business of felling willow trees. These can be anything from a mere 10 trees in one particular location to an estate of between 100 to 150 trees. These may be spread all over the different parts of an estate. Our felling tools may be all manner of implements, with a variety of shapes and sizes, ropes and vehicles to gain access and for the felling. We rely heavily on the modern chain saw which we have to ensure is in prime condition before every single felling expedition.

Chains must be maintained to peak sharpness and engines regularly serviced. It is hazardous and downright inefficient to tackle the task of felling a large number of trees without these prerequisites. Just imagine a situation where a tree is located in an awkward position, having arrived at the point of finally felling it, the engine suddenly fails! Can you visualise the scene? "Sorry, Lord Rochester, there's this willow tree on your best barn" or "Please, can you call the Electricity Board, our tree is through your power cables." How utterly unprofessional! I have said this before, "Leave it to the Professionals". If all and sundry could avoid the commonplace situation I have described, every layman would be an expert Professional!

The tree is now felled and lying horizontally, ready to be cut into lengths of 28 inches. Why 28 inches in particular? Cricket Bat Willow is essentially a very soft wood, which in its green state tends to split easily. If we allow the original length to be 28 inches, a cricket bat blade is 22 and a quarter inches long, and it is therefore wise to allow five and three quarter inches for any end splits that may occur (Figs. 76, 77 & 78).

Fig. 76 Felled timber

Fig. 77 Creme de la Creme

Fig. 78 Lengthed timber

We measure the length of the tree trunk first, having cleared away any top branches. Normally, such a tree will yield 3 or 4 lengths of 28 inches each. Occasionally a tree may yield a possible 5 lengths of prime timber, of which the first two or even three are capable of producing Cricket Bat Willow's equivalent of '*La Creme de la Creme*', the highly vaunted white wood which is the substance of best bats. What I have described is a utopian ideal, a Cricket Bat Willow grower's pipe dream. If only all willow trees were the same! What if the tree is not straight, or that there is a blemish or a knot midway on the trunk, just because the grower was negligent in his care of the tree in its formative years. He forgot to rub off a bud, which ultimately grew to the size and thickness of a human thumb. It might have been a careless farmer who ran his tractor into the tree, or the chap who trimmed the hedge, and whilst pondering to enjoy a fag, stuck his reaphook into the tree!

Now you can see my point. We have to negotiate our way through all these concerns, when purchasing trees for felling. All trees may seem at face value to be the same, but on deeper and a more thorough examination may reveal all or some of the symptoms I have described. An issue such as late pruning, is one factor that remains hidden as the tree grows on. There is nothing more disappointing than to discover the beautiful sight of a perfect white round which, on splitting, displays Fourth Grade or common timber. Why? All because somebody forgot to rub the buds off in the early spring and late summer.

To get back to our prostrate tree. It has now become 4 or 5 rounds, standing on their ends waiting to be marked out (Fig. 79).

Fig. 79 Marking out end of rounds

Fig. 80 Plastic wedges inserted by D. A. W.

Fig. 81 Wedges in place

Fig. 82 'Beetle' for striking wedges

Fig. 83 Marked out clefts prior to splitting out

Fig. 84 Splitting out with wedges in place

This is done using a razor sharp axe. Plastic wedges are then inserted into the lines marked out by the axe (Figs. 80 & 81). They are then struck with a 'Beetle' (Fig. 82) or the back of an axe so that they drive into the willow tree round, until they cause a split from their entry point to the ground. We call a split borne out of a willow tree a 'cleft'. These are then sawn out, and graded into cricket bat grades, that is to say, Superbest, Best, Seconds, Thirds, Fourths and Boys. Let me elaborate on each grade:

Fig. 85 Grading of sawn clefts
Left to Right:
Superbest, Best, Seconds, Thirds, Fourths, Boys

Superbest: All white, perfectly straight, almost parallel grain, with no marks or blemishes of any kind (Fig. 86).
Best: These may also be all white, but may show a slight deviation in the grain and display a slight colour on the edge (Fig. 87).
Seconds: Predominantly straight grained, but with up to an inch of colour on the edge of the blade (Fig. 88).
Thirds: Displaying half colour and half white (Fig. 89).
Fourths or Common: Precisely what the description suggests, uneven grain, full of colour and heavily stained. The 'Village slogger' type bat! (Fig. 90)

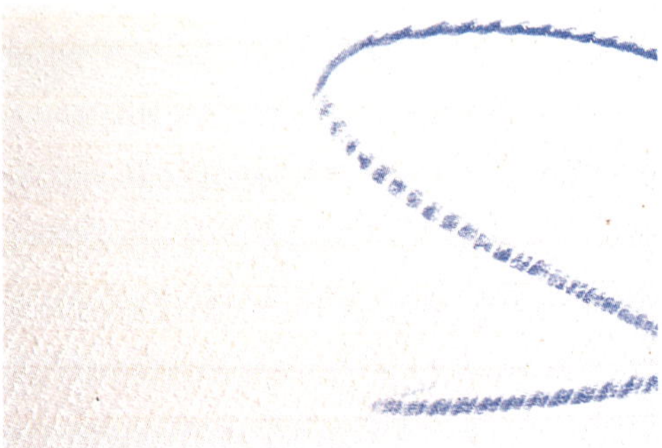

Fig. 86 Superbest

Fig. 87 Best

Fig. 88 Seconds

Fig. 89 Thirds

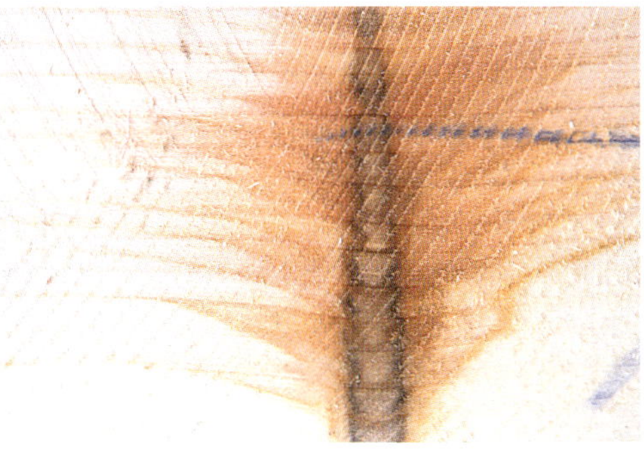

Fig. 90 Fourths

Fig. 91 Boys

Boys: Displaying a cross section of all the men's grades but slightly smaller; men's size clefts are five inches wide when sawn; the boys size is four and a half inches wide (Fig. 91).

These are then carefully dipped at their ends into wax in order to prevent premature splitting from occurring during the drying process (Fig. 92).

Fig. 92 Wax dipping ends of clefts to reduce end splits

Fig. 93 Dried clefts awaiting shipment

They are then transferred into a Dry Kiln, where under carefully and methodically controlled drying, their moisture content is brought down to an optimum level of 14%. The operative word is '*controlled drying*', which has to be adhered to strictly in order to achieve a successfully dried cleft. In our case, we then load 5,000 clefts into a container and ship it to Melbourne, Australia (Figs 93 & 94).

Fig. 94 Kiln and Air dried clefts

One last afterthought, before I bring this chapter to a close. Do you recall my suggestion that trees which are ready for felling should achieve a girth circumference of 56/58 inches at chest height? You may ask what becomes of those trees which exceed that circumference.

Fig. 95 Splitting out including 'inside' splits

Ultra large trees provide, in addition to normal splits, "inside splits". Take the case of a huge tree that will yield between 15 to 20 bats from the outside of the round. This will leave the inner core of the timber from which even more bats can be made. These will display all the characteristics of fullness of colour, and therefore be graded as common fourths for men's bats and for boy's bats. Let me assure you that commercial pressures are such in the current bat-making climate that there is always demand for even the inside splits – our constant problem remains in fulfilling it.

CHAPTER 8

THE MANUFACTURE OF THE BAT

The bat making industry today bears scant resemblance to what it was in the days when my Father was alive. Tools such as 'the drawknife', 'the spokeshave', 'the hand hammer' and 'the box plane' have assumed *Neanderthal* status in the bat making industry today (Figs. 96, 97, 98 & 99).

Fig. 96 Box plane (photo – courtesy of Messrs Warsop-Stebbing, Danbury)

Let me take you back to those times. Imagine this scene. The cleft, having been cut to length, with a preliminary shape already carved. We are about to proceed to the real task of shaping and balancing the bat. The splice has been sawn out, by hand of course, with the handle inserted and fitted using good old carpenter's glue. This glue is different from modern synthetic glues, in that it was derived from animal products and available in sheets that resembled brown toffee. They were translucent, and available in sheets of one square foot or a little more. These would be crumbled into a pot, which would then be placed in a larger pot containing

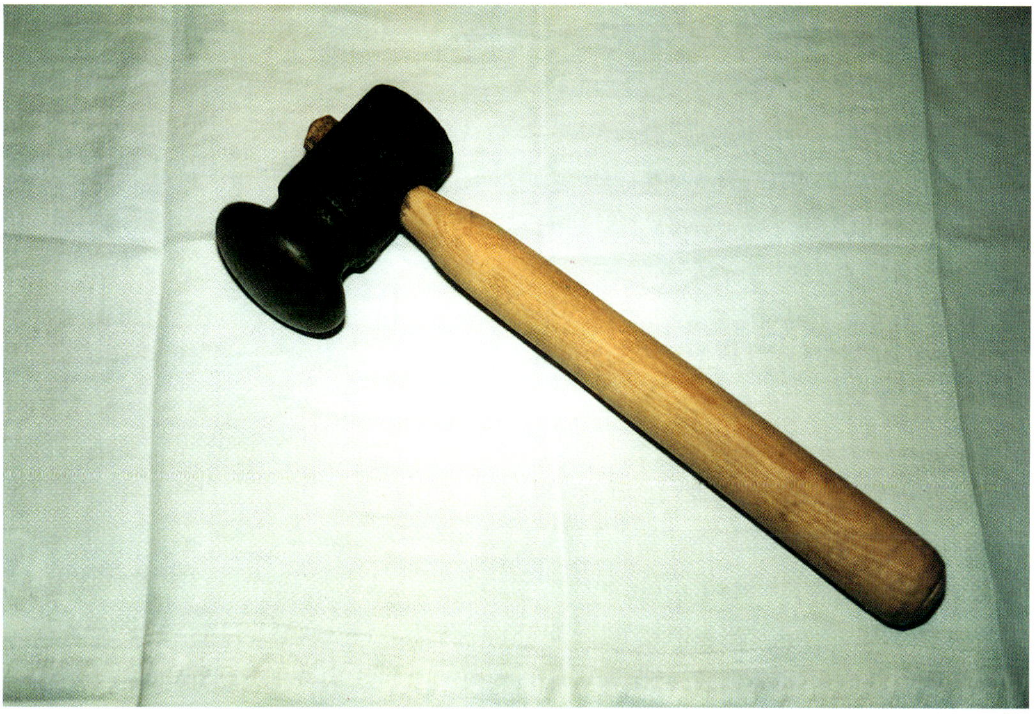

Fig. 97 Hand hammer

Fig. 98 Hand hammer and Drawknife

Fig. 99 Spokeshave

water. The larger pot and its contents would be placed on a gas ring or similar for a long period of time, so that the water would be allowed to boil at a constant heat. The glue in the smaller pot would by now have melted to a liquefied state that you would use for joining the handle into the splice (Fig. 100).

Fig. 100 Old type glue pot (photo – courtesy of Messrs Warsop Stebbing, Danbury)

Our handles were all meticulously hand made in those days. '*Manau*' cane was shipped from Sarawak, in the East Indies, in 12-foot bundles. These bundles were approximately a foot to eighteen inches in circumference, and held together at each end with strong rope resembling coconut twine.

We would then cut these 12 feet lengths into segments, and apportion them in appropriate numbers of Short Handles and Long Handles, varying according to the grade of handle required. The assembly, by hand, of a cricket bat handle was in itself a dedicated craft. It looked more like a work of art and, believe me, it was a labour of love. This is not the case today. (See Chapter 9).

Similarly, the bat would have been carved out with loving care and consummate skill, the face having been planed to perfection, the back drawn, the shoulders and toe shaped, with the handle having been set in the splice using old carpenter's glue. This would lead us to the finishing process, which included 'pressing' the bat (Figs. 101 & 102.

Fig. 101 Face planed, ready for shaping

Fig. 102 Handle fitted into cleft

Pressing a bat? How then were bats 'pressed in' those days? There is still much debate about machine pressing and hand pressing today, so what was it like in those days?

The face of the bat blade would still be as soft as it was when the tree was felled, except that it would be at the correct moisture level now. A cricket ball tossed on to the face of the bat would cause dents in it immediately. The face of a cricket bat is required to be pressed primarily to avoid causing damage to the face and edges of the bat by a cricket ball but it also has a bearing on the way the bat will perform in a cricket match.

The real skill lies in pressing the bat at just the right pressure. Too much pressing and the blade is safe from damage by a cricket ball, but bat makers and top players will tell you that the 'drive' will disappear from the bat. Too little pressing will lead to damage by a cricket ball. Today, a good bat maker will press the bat just enough on the face and edges, so that the bat retains its natural 'drive'.

Gray-Nicolls press at 200lbs per square inch. Systems vary because of inconsistency in graining and density. The user is then required to continue the pressing by a process of 'knocking the bat in'. This is done by many users by continuously tapping an old cricket ball on the bat or by discerning cricketers knocking the face of the blade using a special mallet made from either of the two hardwoods, Ash or Lignum Vitae. I personally do not agree with this practice of tampering by amateurs!

Pressing machines were at an embryonic stage then, and most knowledgeable bat makers resorted to laborious 'hand hammering'. I witnessed my Father take a bat blade set in a 'V' shaped wooden jig, to rest the back of the bat in and thus expose the full face of the bat, at which he meticulously and systematically struck a set pattern of blows with a hammer (Fig. 103).

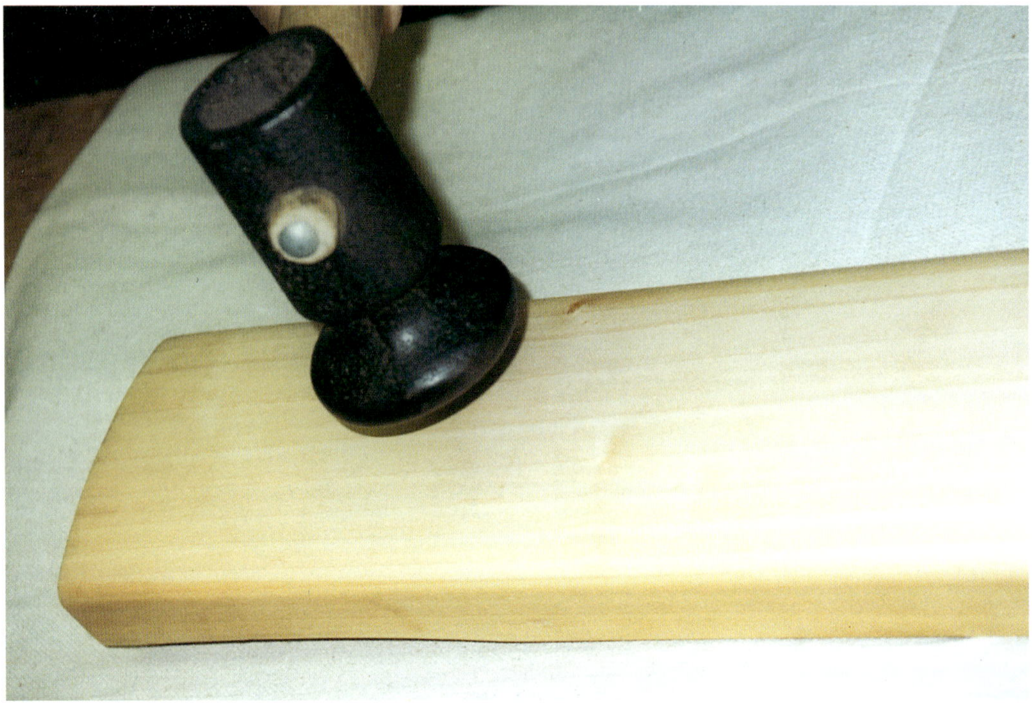

Fig. 103 Hand hammering the blade

This hammer was by its design created to press the face of the bat in a precise and even manner. This process of individual hand pressing was a labour of love as you can imagine. What the hand held hammer performed was automatic quality control in the process of pressing. No two blades of Cricket Bat Willow are ever the same, even from the same tree. There may be more grains in one, less in the other, some areas harder or softer than others. The hand hammering process would use eye and feel to determine uniformity of pressing. A critical issue in pressing done today. Does a machine press that is designed to press a bat uniformly with a weighted roller have eyes like those of a human being, or the sensation of touch? The answer is no. Yesteryear's pressing was done by hand hammering, which was an art form in itself. I should know that, because I have watched my Father and I still have his hand hammer.

The process of shaping the bat using a "drawknife and plane" was under pressure to reform. The pressure was commercially led, as these tools were considered too slow for rising bat demand. Eventually machines were developed and introduced.

A huge machine was built which would accommodate a number of identical lengths of cleft in a row, and after a short sharp unleashing of its programmed cutters, it would produce a number of pre-formed bats which were then pre-pressed before fitting to the handle. The bats still had to be finished by hand. So much then for the time honoured craft of bat making. The tradition, fine tuned over decades, requiring single minded adherence to principles of yesteryear, now exists as a near extinct legacy with a few bat makers who hand craft their bats. These are bat makers like Hassan Mughal, Tim Keeley and a few specialists within Gray-Nicolls, Slazenger and Gunn & Moore.

Just to conclude, and prove a point in question, I have a part made blade of a high quality bat made by Messrs Gray-Nicolls. It displays at its toe a great brown slash revealing the inside of a 'bumknot', running across it (Fig. 104).

The existence of this fault renders the blade unworthy for bat making. However, a good bat maker using a drawknife would have seen the fault and removed it. The

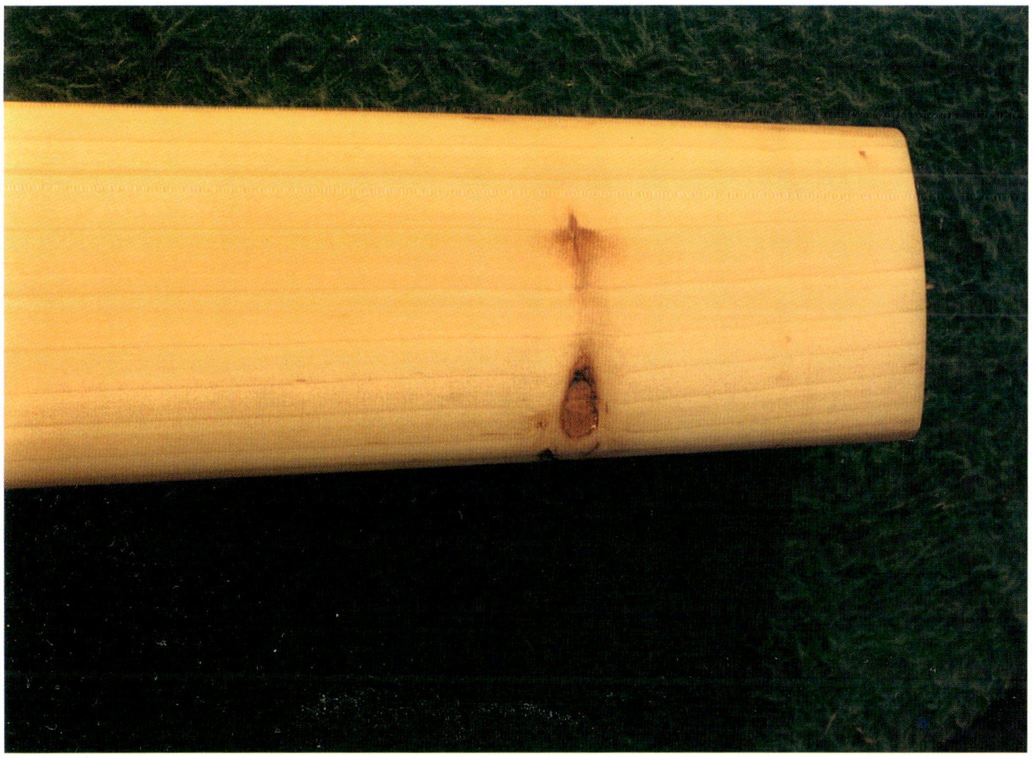

Fig. 104 Bumknot in partly made bat

machine, as I mentioned earlier, neither has eyes to see the 'bumknot', nor the use of a drawknife to extract it. It can only make shapes.

Of the old carpenter's glue . . . I have painful memories. My wrist, to this day, bears the scars of a brushful of boiling glue that indisposed me for a full week . . . and they talk of the "good old days".

CHAPTER 9

THE HANDLE

Whilst I have maintained the importance of knowing the grading process in the Cricket Bat Willow cleft, the 'handle' is equally important and in many ways a complex entity within its own right. I hope that by discussing the grading system of the *Salix Alba*, most discerning cricket followers will be able to distinguish types of grade with relative ease and knowledge, to their own benefit.

Would they be as conversant with such a vastly diverse topic as the handle? Just as in the case of Cricket Bat Willow, there are numerous considerations to take into account. For example, these are just some of the questions asked. Where does the handle come from? – Are there different grades of handle? – How is it assembled? – What are 'springs'? – What is the length of the handle? – How is it fitted? – Does it ever break? – Why . . . The list is both complex and endless. Each question should be viewed in the context of the following backdrop.

The handle is constructed meticulously using 'pre-cut' splines of 'MANAU' cane that grows in its natural habitat in Sarawak, in the Eastern Malaysian State of Borneo. It was customary, during my early experience of bat making, that cane was imported in bundles directly from Sarawak. Most handles were individually customised in a bespoke fashion to fulfil individual demand. Nowadays, handles are available which have been made *en masse* without honouring the time consuming craft which my Father first introduced me to. Naturally, making handles *en masse* somehow defies rigorous quality control, and the photographs below reveal some of the defects in mass produced handles.

Fig. 105 Handle defects

Fig. 106 Damaged handles

You may have your own particular experience relating to the performance or rather the behaviour of some bat whose handle broke in some past game of cricket. I can recall one particular game which I was enjoying watching on the television. The batsman played a flourishing full blooded cover drive with a massive follow through of the bat over his shoulder . . . except, in this instance his bat took off rocketing over the 'mid off' area, whilst the handle remained firmly held by the batsman!

In this instance, the break probably occurred due to faulty gluing of the handle to the splice. I have seen, on many other occasions handles breaking cleanly at the point just above the 'shoulders' of the bat. In several games that I have watched, such mishaps have been treated with instantaneous mirth and ribaldry. Comments such as "My boomerang won't come back" and "Did it catch the ball?" have sent titters around the ground!

The handle can break in several different places and in many different ways. Much, of course, depends on the player, the standard of play he is involved in, and the area of the bat where greatest stress is exerted (Figs. 105 & 106).

You will have noticed in games of cricket, young, strapping, strong lads, almost leaning on the bat, whist taking stance at the crease. There is a tendency for some to bend the bat down, put pressure on it, and some lean on it so hard that the handle will bend. This is done almost subconsciously, as if to reassure the batsman that the handle and the bat are strong!

When you examine the precise construction of the handle, and this can be done by pulling one to pieces, you will notice the following. The handle displays a set (the number can vary according to the bat maker's preference) of cubed pre-cut lengths of cane which have been joined together with glue. The canes are separated by pre-inserted lengths of rubber, felt, or cork, or a combination of any or all of these. This set of inserts creates flexibility or 'springs' in the handle. Once these elements have been joined together they form the basis of a handle, but in their unfinished state resemble a long cube. The number of canes can vary, according to the strength and flexibility required in the handle. The variation can span between 1 or 2 pieces of cane creating a basic but strong handle, to a superior 12-piece cane handle used in the very top bats.

When the handle has been inserted into the splice it has been turned to a fairly thick finish, with enough thickness to allow the bat maker to shape it down to a mass or individual requirement. The shape can be achieved by turning the bat handle through a lathe and leaving it round, as was the custom in the old days, or a good bat maker will rasp the handle down for feel and shape using a metal rasp. The fashion in recent years has been to shape the bottom of the handle oval.

To revert back to the batsman who habitually leans on his bat, his actions will put large amounts of concerted pressure on the bat handle. Remember it is designed to complement the blade, when striking the ball. This causes sudden shock to the bat, but literally only for a split second, as the ball cannons off the face of the bat. This shock is totally different to the one caused by leaning on the bat. The stress that this latter habit creates transmits along the strips of cane, and to the glue that binds them, along its length, causing the bond between the cane strips to 'give' and then eventually capitulate by separating the strips. This leads to the eventual collapse of the handle. I have witnessed some horrendous looking handles, which have led me to wonder how they came to be in that condition.

It is fascinating to think just for a moment, what happens to a bat and handle in matches where a ball thunders in to the bat at speeds of around 100 miles per hour. The 'G-Force' factor, for a split second, is such that the bat has to repel the ball with force that is equal to that of the ball travelling towards the bat. In cricket, they refer to a batsman 'timing' the ball, which in practice means the bat meeting the ball with split second opposite force. You can imagine the cumulative stress which repeated batting places not only on the blade, but more so on the handle. It speaks volumes regarding the inherent resilience of the Cricket Bat Willow. I know of no other species of wood that copes as well with such stress factors.

The handle of the bat has to be examined continuously, with feel and visible signs of weakening detected as early as possible. In such cases, it should be returned to any good bat maker who will replace the handle. A more common situation is one where a handle has been extremely well cared for, but where the blade becomes damaged. Again, a reputable bat maker will 're-blade' the handle at reasonable cost, leaving you with an almost new bat.

A final note, before concluding this chapter. Handles come in all lengths, as follows: Supershort (10 inches), Short (11 inches), Long (12 inches). Always take advice on the correct size of handle, and use one that *you* are most comfortable with, and do not under any circumstances follow the "I play with what I am given" caveat. With any young player it could spell the end of a promising career.

CHAPTER 10

DISTRIBUTION

In this, the penultimate chapter of '**The Life and Times of the Cricket Bat Willow**', I shall cover the important area of distributing Cricket Bat Willow, which for us at Anglian Willow Service has become a way of life.

What I am about to say will, I believe, surprise and confound you. Can you believe that the counties of Essex, Suffolk and Norfolk are responsible for supplying the greatest proportion of Cricket Bat Willow to the entire world? There are some isolated pockets of Cricket Bat Willow grown as far afield as Dorset, Yorkshire and Herefordshire. These are, however, of minor importance and really insignificant when considered within the total scale of distribution of *Salix Alba Caerulea.* The county of Essex alone, produces by far the best and the largest proportion of willow of any of the three counties mentioned.

You may ask how other countries get their Cricket Bat Willow and if, as I have said in earlier chapters, the trees can be grown, why can't other countries grow their own supply? The answer is two fold. First, the soil types are not suitable, and second, the climatic conditions are not ideal for successful growth.

I have discussed in an earlier chapter of this book that the ideal distance between growth lines on the face of a bat should be approximately half an inch, with some degree of uniformity. In order to achieve this, a tree needs to grow at a consistent annual rate for a period of between 12 and 15 years. If this period is interrupted by, say, a drought (as was the case in 1995/6) then this will create a growth line of about one quarter of an inch on the face of the bat, which rather puts the cat among the pigeons so far as uniformity of growth is concerned. However, such is the way of nature.

If we take the discussion regarding growing conditions further, what about cricket playing countries such as New Zealand, and some areas of Australia or any country with a similar climate to that of the United Kingdom? There is justification in giving some consideration to these arguments.

I visited Australia in 1994 and had the pleasure of meeting the Minister of Agriculture, who went to great lengths to persuade me to take up residence in Australia for a period of ten years, so that I could oversee a programme of growing Cricket Bat Willow. I gave him various genuine objections against the move, that of age (I was 72 at the time), the strict immigration laws and other pressing commitments. He smiled, and replied, "Doug, if you'll come, there is no obstacle".

I am a converted Aussie at heart, and I find the climate, the people, and the sheer scale and beauty of the outback fascinating. Nothing would have given me more pleasure than to start an exciting project in such marvellous surroundings. I had to regrettably decline the offer on several grounds, one of which is the fact that my son Geoffrey is a full partner in the business, and I could not let him down. Instead, I came back home, and decided to write this book.

Believe me, I'll be back at the first opportunity – I love Australia. Apart from which, there is a young man over there following the guidelines I gave him. In ten to twelve years time he may be a saviour to Australian cricket, providing them with home grown timber. I wish him well in his endeavours.

I have mentioned New Zealand, in an earlier paragraph, in view of its milder climatic conditions. I am due to make a visit there in 1996/97 in order to inspect potential Cricket Bat Willow growing sites. In the meantime, I will take you back to our willow which we ship out to Melbourne. We do this by packing up to 5,000 clefts of willow into a large shipping container. Prior to this the clefts have to be dried, either naturally or by kilning, down to 14% moisture content or less. This is the case with all exported Cricket Bat Willow. This container is fumigated, sealed

Fig. 107 Container arriving at Gray-Nicolls, Melbourne, Australia

and certificated, then loaded on to the ship which, 'Conference' or 'Non Conference,' will reach Melbourne in between 5 and 7 weeks of sailing. The same system of shipping applies wherever you export Cricket Bat Willow, or for that matter any other matter that is shipped in a similar manner (Fig. 107).

There are one or two problems which can occur en route, which must be mentioned – mostly concerned with 'filthy lucre'.

As with export of any type, it is common commercial practice nowadays, to receive payment in advance before goods that you have sent are released to the recipient from Customs. One method is to ensure that you are in possession of a Bankers Draft, the other, becoming more common, is an Irrevocable Letter of Credit (ILC) issued by the importers bank in your favour before goods are dispatched. Just a little warning . . . there have been exceptions.

In most cases our trade with our overseas clients has proceeded smoothly apart from the odd minor hiccup. Some years ago, however, details of 'sharp' dealing came to our notice in connection with the make-up of bats delivered abroad for manufacturing into 'boys' bats.

Now in order to understand that situation you need to know that when we prepare clefts for making into men's bats, these are sawn to a width of five inches. The same is not the case for clefts used for making 'boys' bats. Theses are sawn to a width of four and a half inches. When you consider that after the finishing process, a man's bat is four and one eighth of an inch wide, it does not take great guesswork to create, albeit with great care, a man's bat from a boy's cleft. It is possible to achieve this, but in my experience only those of ill repute and peddling uncouth practices would indulge in this type of business. They may argue that they are simply exploiting a situation which is presented to them. I may add, though, that the thickness of a boy's cleft is less than that of a man's cleft. While it may produce *a man's size bat*, the bat maker will encounter problems in carving a top class shape from the cleft (Fig. 108).

Fig. 108 Difference between mens and boys bats

I feel this practice is a matter of personal choice, and if someone came and regularly asked me to quote for parcels of boys' size clefts sawn to four and three quarters of an inch, then I would, without hesitation, quote men's clefts prices. It really depends on each individual case in question.

If we revert back to one of the repeated problems of distribution of Cricket Bat Willow by sea, you will encounter extremes of hot and cold on a journey taking the container from the Northern Hemisphere port of Felixstowe, to Melbourne in the Southern Hemisphere. During its voyage the ship will transcend in a southerly direction, the Tropic of Cancer, the Equator, and the Tropic of Capricorn, and several climatic changes en route. If the container is carried above deck on the ship, the process of heating within the container will cause clefts to split in what we term as 'sweating up'.

In any one trip of the type described above, I have heard it mentioned in cricket bat making circles that losses of up to 15% due to 'splits' are quite commonplace. One has, therefore, got to grant the poor bat maker some sympathy as he may have to deal with bat returns on an epidemic scale, caused as a result of the voyage and gross mishandling.

A general note on damage, not relating to causation during distribution. On numerous occasions I have seen bat faces mutilated . . . as a result of stumps being knocked in to the ground using the bat face. Also, more commonly, the end of a bat handle being used to knock in stumps. *This is wrong* and should be avoided at all times. There are proper tools for the job, such as a specially made 'stump mallet'. I can remember terrible damage being inflicted on bat faces and handles when stumps had brass ferrules around the tops.

Fig. 109 Mutilated bat faces

The same goes for all you 'sloggers' out there, who are reading this. If you find that your bat suffers a broken corner at the toe, it is more likely to be the result of an injudicious wild smash, rather than a properly executed stroke. In cases where flaws to bats are caused by an inherent defect in the wood, or there is a problem in the workmanship, bat makers in most cases will be happy to rectify these. Such however, is the nature of the game of cricket, that sometimes the line between genuine damage and negligently caused damage can be a very fine one. Do not therefore, be surprised if the bat maker's patience is tested sorely in these circumstances!

CHAPTER 11

Choosing a Bat

This is **the** million-dollar question that continues to confound and daunt most cricket bat buyers. Imagine this scenario, and see if you have either experienced it yourself, or heard of it. Does it sound familiar?

The cricket season is near, the young boy, a keen cricketer, needs a new bat, and thinks that he knows a thing or two about bats. He badgers his father into submission, and drags him along to the nearest sports shop. The father professes to be a minor authority on the topic as well. They arrive at the shop only to be met by the salesman who is as keen as mustard to take the father's money and encourage him to spend the maximum amount. I am not suggesting for one instance that the salesman is a shark – but there are salesmen and there are salesmen.

Fig. 110 Bat range

The commercial pressure is such on sports shops in these competitive times, that customer service, and in particular relating to the potential purchase of a cricket bat has taken a back seat. You cannot make a proper considered decision by hurrying the selecting and buying process. It was customary in times gone by when the salesman would invite you to the shop, and lead you to the bat rack and say, "Now then, sir, let's try a few for weight, size, balance, and general feel. Let's also establish whether you need a long handle or a short handle".

This is in complete and stark contrast to what I encountered on an occasion one Christmas, when I went to a shop and inquired, "I'd like to buy a cricket bat for this young man", only to be met by, "Over there mate . . . . in the rack on the wall". How then, does one proceed to conduct a satisfactory purchase of a cricket bat?

First decide beforehand, certain basic tenets, by looking round the rack. See if you can recognise some of the reputable bat makes. . . . Is there one similar to the one you currently own . . . who was it made by? What was the weight and size? Was it perfectly suited to your type of play? Were you completely satisfied with it or did you want one lighter, a little heavier perhaps, with a good pick up, perhaps more equally balanced or bottom heavy? These are many questions. Keep asking and reminding yourself of *your own requirements*. Take your time. Above all, do not be hurried or pushed. It is vitally imperative that if it is talent that you have, then you must satisfy yourself. It is your cricketing future that is at stake. Remember the Brian Lara story in the first chapter . . . he thought that he had the right bat . . . changed it to one that felt better, the result is history and etched forever in the annals of cricket history books.

It so happens that we supply Cricket Bat Willow to Messrs Gray-Nicolls with some of the finest quality willow in the world. I have always been associated with and been synonymous with quality where Cricket Bat Willow is concerned. I believe Gray-Nicolls are the biggest manufacturers and suppliers of cricket bats in the world today. Their bats make up over 70% of the cricket bat supply market in the world – but small can be beautiful as well, and there are some fine individual bat makers coming along . . . Tim Keeley of Newbery Bats and Hassan Mughal of Imperial Bats . . . watch them.

There you have the crux of several questions which are a must, when seeking to buy a new cricket bat – but the choice is entirely yours. If you ever require personal service, whether it is for advice on Cricket Bat Willow or related matters, we will be delighted to help you select your blade from our extensive stocks of top quality willow. You may then take this to a quality bat maker who will hand craft the bat precisely according to your individual specifications – how's that for personal service?

Fig. 111 Doug Watling with his son Geoffrey who is in the process of assuming the reins of the business to ensure continuity

Finally, for the last word on *Salix Alba Caerulea*, subject of this book – '**The Life and Times of the Cricket Bat Willow**'. If you grow it, contact us – we believe you will be pleasantly surprised. Let us face it, 4 generations of expertise are not to be sneezed at!

I remain at your disposal, in that it is my pleasure to enjoy your company anywhere within the United Kingdom to conduct lectures and demonstrations, and lectures only anywhere in the world, upon receipt of suitable invitation and notification.

Always at your service.

Internet World Wide Web Site

Information on the business activities of ANGLIAN WILLOW SERVICE and this book, 'The Life and Times of the Cricket Bat Willow' will be available world wide on the Internet.

Access to the WWW Site can be gained by keying the commands in the 'Home' page of the readers Internet software.

The Internet site will be available via all Search Engines. Users should type any or all of the following words: Cricket, Bats, Anglian Willow, Willow, books.

Alternatively, a WWW site address can be gained by contacting the Author or Publisher of this book.

Lectures and Demonstrations

It has been customary for Doug Watling to attend the most important County Shows within and adjacent to the County of Essex. In addition to exhibiting at these outdoor events, Doug is often invited to speak at 'After Dinner' functions at a vast array of important occasions.

Doug usually starts with the splitting of a 'round' of willow using an axe and wedges, into first stage clefts. These are shown with the various gradings from Super Best down to Boys. The discussion becomes a two-way exchange of views on the various grades. The last part of the demonstration involves discussion on bat making and exhibiting a full range of cricket bats (including one signed by Brian Lara commemorating his World Test Record score of 375, achieved at Antigua in 1994).

Full details of the fee structure relating to demonstrations in the UK and lectures world-wide is available from Anglian Willow Service. Copies of this book for sale and personally signed by Doug are available at the end of the show.

DOCUMENTARY FILM

The Life and Times of the Cricket Bat Willow

A short subject film documentary using the subject matter of the book will be commissioned in late 1998.

'The Life and Times of the Cricket Bat Willow' will be commissioned into a short subject film in late 1998.

The subject matter of the book will form the basis of a 30-40 minute film documentary under the Sole and Exclusive Copyright of Douglas A.Watling. The film will be available to all interested parties and will be particularly suitable for special subject programming on Inflight TV as well as terrestrial Television.

Full Details of Transmission Fees and availability are available from:

ANGLIAN WILLOW SERVICE,
4 Chevers Hall Cottage,
Chelmsford Road,
High Ongar,
ESSEX, CM5 9NX (UK)
Tel/Fax: +44 1277 363950

'The Life and Times of The Cricket Bat Willow'

A Walk in the Countryside

A peace - a quiet, almost reverential peace - seemed to pervade the area I had entered.

There were trees on all sides. Large and small, all reaching for the blue of the sunlit sky. It was midsummer and all was green and vibrant with life and living. The tall heads of these seemingly delicate examples of forestry, or organised growth, swayed gently in a light wind and sighed with an almost human sound suggestive of reassuring, comforting aura of "be at peace, all is well here"

Following my leisurely steps my gaze enveloped a slowly winding stream wending its way through beds of water lilies and other flora and fauna, adding to the feel of these beautiful surroundings. Indeed, were I not involved in a business sense, I could quite easily have sat by this beautiful stream in this patch of wonderful British countryside and developed the theme, "Where else could you find such a glorious spot?"

My reverie was shattered by the sound of a voice claiming my attention with a query about one of the trees around us.

It was my son, Geoff - we own the land on which I stood and dreamed...and the trees - all magnificent specimens - we were choosing this year's crop of potential Cricket Bats for the Brian Lara's and the Mark Ramprakash's of this world.

Ah well...back to reality!

D.A.W.

INDEX OF FIGURES